UnCivil Servant

Holding Government Employees Accountable

William B. Wiley
Deborah J. Hopkins
Attorneys at Law

ISBN 978-0-9729852-0-8

Distributed by the
Federal Employment Law Training Group, LLC

www.FELTG.com

CONTENTS

UNCIVIL SERVANT

Holding Government Employees Accountable
for
Performance and Conduct

William B. Wiley

Deborah J. Hopkins

Attorneys at Law

This text is devoted to the principle of increasing government productivity by raising employee accountability while scrupulously protecting employee legal rights.

About the Authors

William Wiley began his federal government career in 1967 as a summer intern working in the House of Representatives. In 1968, while still in college, he began working part-time in the Executive Branch as a GS-4 Cotton Insect Research Technician for the US Department of Agriculture. He completed his federal Executive Branch career in 2002 as a member of the Senior Executive Service holding the position of Chief Counsel to the Chairman of the U.S. Merit Systems Protection Board (MSPB).

After obtaining his Bachelor of Science degree in 1970, Mr. Wiley served on active duty in the U.S. Navy. Upon discharge from the Navy, he utilized the G.I. bill educational benefit to obtain a Master of Science degree in Organizational Psychology. That degree allowed him to enter the field of Human Resources as a GS-7 labor/employee relations specialist for the Naval Regional Medical Center, San Diego. After being promoted within Navy to the position of Regional Employee Relations Advisor, he received his first Presidential appointment under President Ronald Reagan to be an advisor to a member of MSPB in Washington, D.C. Subsequently, President H.W. Bush appointed him as Chief of Staff to the General Counsel of the Federal Labor Relations Authority (FLRA). Upon his election, President Bill Clinton appointed Mr. Wiley to be the Chief Counsel to the Chairman of MSPB, a position in which he served for eight years. Finally, under President G.W. Bush, he served as Chief Counsel to the Vice Chairman of MSPB.

Upon leaving government in 2002, Mr. Wiley co-founded the Federal Employment Law Training Group, LLC. He served as its President through 2018.

In 1989, Mr. Wiley became an attorney by passing the California bar exam without the benefit of attending law school. Today, he is in the private practice of law in San Francisco, California. He represents agencies throughout government in all areas of civil service law.

Deborah Hopkins is the President of the Federal Employment Law Training Group. She graduated cum laude from the University of the District of Columbia – David A. Clarke School of Law, and is admitted to practice law in the District of Columbia. She has worked on cases before the U.S. Merit Systems Protection Board and the U.S. Equal Employment Opportunity Commission. She has also worked with the Government Accountability Project (GAP), a public-interest non-partisan whistleblower protection and advocacy organization. Ms. Hopkins has over 15 years of experience in adult education and training.

Before becoming an attorney, Ms. Hopkins was Training Manager at LRP Publications/cyberFEDS®. She has presented training sessions to thousands of federal employees in the HR, ER, LR, EEO, civil rights, legal writing and supervisory arenas. She has developed courses and authored a number of training manuals for institutions of higher education. She was also co-author of the fourth edition of *UnCivil Servant: Holding Government Employees Accountable for Performance and Conduct* (Dewey Publications, 2016).

UNCIVIL SERVANT

We, the authors, dedicate this book to every hard-working, honest, civil servant in government everywhere.

We would not have a society without you.

Thank you.

PROLOGUE

Do not skip this section. Yes, we know; most prologues are meaningless dribble about the authors or unnecessary ruminations about the meaning of life. However, this prologue is different because you need to keep some very timely matters in mind as you read this text.

First, if you work at the Department of Veterans Affairs (VA), you need to be aware that in June of 2017, Congress changed the accountability laws that apply to your employees by approving the "Department of Veterans Affairs Accountability and Whistleblower Protection Act of 2017." Unlike most other agencies, VA now has regular civil service employees whose rights are defined by this legislation, Title 38 employees, "hybrid" employees that fall into more than one category, and goodness knows how many other categories of employment. Each of these groups has different procedural and appeal rights, deceptively similar, but ultimately different in application and possible outcome.

This text does NOT go into the details of these differences and does NOT claim to accurately describe the changes that were promulgated by the 2017 act. The main reason we chose not to go into details relative to these changes is that they have not yet been litigated in court and there are currently pending significant legal challenges to their Constitutionality and their application. If we were to claim to know what they mean now before the courts have had a chance to consider them, we might be misleading those readers who do not have the most recent edition of this text. However, in broadly stated language, here are some of the major changes:

- The minimum time period required for firing a bad employee has been reduced by about 25%.

- The amount of proof necessary for a supervisor on appeal to prove that removal is warranted has been reduced from "removal is *probably* warranted" to "removal *might be* warranted" (more on the burdens of proof in civil service law in later chapters).

- Supervisors no longer have to defend their decisions to remove an employee rather than impose a lesser level of discipline (e.g., a suspension). Judges reviewing these cases on appeal can no longer rule that a removal is too severe and should be mitigated to a lower penalty.

Hopefully, by the time we produce the next edition of *UnCivil Servant*, we'll be able to flesh out the newly-developed procedures at VA.

Of course, most readers are not VA supervisors. Most of you work at other agencies. Why should you care what has happened with this new legislation? Well, for one big fat reason: President Trump said in his 2018 State of the Union address that he believes that the VA changes should be applied throughout government. And in his 2019 budget proposal for the Executive Branch, he proposed that changes similar to those made for the VA be incorporated by law for all other federal agencies.

Things don't get into a State of the Union address or budget proposal by accident. There has to be an intent to make them happen and sponsors working to put changes into law and regulation. Even with a divided government or even with a different President, there is an enduring amount of bipartisan support for changing the law to make it easier for federal supervisors to fire unproductive and misbehaving federal workers. Like it or not, we have to accept that there is a good possibility of legislative action intended to incorporate all or parts of the statutory changes implemented at the VA in 2017 into the rest of the government.

Separately, in May of 2018, the President exercised his authority to direct his secretaries and department heads via Executive Order (EO) to tighten up their utilization of existing law to make it easier to fire bad federal employees (EO 13839). We will highlight and detail those EO directives for you in the following chapters. Again, in broad summary, they are:

- Restrict the time for making a decision on a proposed removal from unlimited to 30 days. The law since 1978 has required a *minimum* of 30 days. Unfortunately, some agencies have been taking months (and even YEARS!) to issue a final decision on a proposed removal.

- Clarify that progressive discipline is not required prior to firing a bad employee.

- Clarify that a prior act of discipline (e.g. a Reprimand for Insubordination) can be considered a prior act of discipline for the purpose of applying the principle of progressive discipline even if the subsequent act of misconduct is of another type (e.g. the second act of misconduct is Disrespectful Conduct).

- Clarify that supervisors are not limited to initiating a level of discipline no higher than that ever taken anywhere else within the agency for the same misconduct.

- Clarify that when an employee is performing unacceptably, the supervisor can institute immediately a 30-day period for the employee to demonstrate whether he can actually perform at an acceptable level, then propose to remove the employee at the end of the period if he fails. This Presidential directive does away with the concept of allowing an employee a period to "improve" performance prior to termination. It also restricts the demonstration period generally to 30 days. Some agencies had been allowing several months for "improvement" prior to initiating a proposed removal.

Separately, as of this writing we have endured over two years without a quorum of members at the U.S. Merit Systems Protection Board. Normally, MSPB would be issuing four or five decisions every business day, most involving appeals of terminations from federal employment, as it has for nearly 40 years. Each of those decisions adds to the body of caselaw that provides guidance to federal supervisors and employment law practitioners when dealing with a problem employee. The Board being effectively shut down has deprived us all of precedential decisions that would help both agencies and employees understand and operate within the civil service system.

These are the most tumultuous times we have had in civil service employment law in over 40 years. We are seeing permanent changes to employee rights and management obligations in some agencies via legislation, perhaps temporary emphasis and instruction via EO, and an ongoing active dialogue as to just what our civil service should look like. Should federal employees have significant rights that hinder the ability of their agency to hold them accountable? Or, should federal supervisors be provided procedures that allow for the prompt low-effort removal of misbehaving or non-productive civil servants?

Answers to these questions will be made in the future by officials at higher pay grades than those held by the authors of this textbook. As will always be our advice in challenging times like these, find advisors you can trust and rely on them to keep you current on the law.

A Note on Personal Pronouns

The English language lacks a third person singular pronoun universally interpreted to be sex neutral. Although we are not comfortable with the convention, this text will default to using "he" and related pronouns as other options are often distracting, and because that is the convention currently used by many courts and administrative bodies. We welcome suggestions regarding pronoun use for future editions.

And, no, we will not use an unmarked plural pronoun with a singular antecedent. Some things just are not right.

QUICK START

Firing a government employee can be very complicated and time-consuming if you do not know what you are doing. Much of this text is devoted to helping you understand those complexities and dealing with them in a straightforward efficient manner. However, with the many permutations and options aside, there is a single direct way that any government employee can be fired.

In some ways, we hesitate to present this section to you because a supervisor really needs to know the theory of discipline and the various tools that are available for dealing with a problem employee that make up the bulk of this text. At the same time, we realize that many of you will benefit from knowing a guaranteed simplified approach for dealing with a problem employee that will withstand review in any forum (as long as your motives are above reproach and your heart is pure). You may have grievances and complaints filed against you, but just consider them as the slings and arrows you must endure to clear the hurdles that lie before you. Although we highly recommend you study and understand the substantive chapters of this book before embarking on a course to remove a government employee, here is the most direct path to dealing with a problem employee that will always result in a successful termination. Some might call this the chapter the "Keys to the Kingdom," but we steal a concept from the computer world and just call it Quick Start:

Step One: Give the employee an order. Put it in writing, be specific, and set a time for performance.

Step Two: If the employee obeys the order in the time specified, you don't have a problem employee, at least not as far as this order is concerned. Go find something else to do with your leadership skills. Assuming that this guy really is a loser, he will not comply within the time frame you established, so Step Two is: Issue a Letter of Reprimand for "Failing to Comply with an Order."

Step Three: Give the employee another order with a time frame for compliance. When the employee does not obey, propose a one to five work day suspension for "Failure to Comply with an Order – second offense." The length of the suspension will be determined by the harm the agency suffered because of the failure to comply. Consult your management advisers and utilize the Douglas Factors you will find discussed later in this text to select an appropriate suspension length.

[In earlier editions of this text, we recommended a second suspension if the employee engages in subsequent misconduct. However, the Government Accountability Office recently has criticized the use of more than one suspension. The theory appears to be a good one: If a first suspension does not motivate an employee to correct his behavior, there's no science that says that a second suspension is any more likely to motivate him to obey the rules. Although this principle has not yet been articulated by the judges who rule in these matters, until someone in authority rules otherwise, we believe that it's safe to use a single suspension prior to a termination.]

Step Four: Give the employee a third order. When the employee does not comply, propose his removal. His pattern of disrespect for authority coupled with your patience and your pattern of progressive discipline will be viewed with respect and admiration by most any arbitrator or administrative judge who hears the appeal of the termination, and the removal will be sustained.

My gosh, this is a lot of steps isn't it? Can't a government employee be fired without having to go through all these reprimands and suspensions? Oh yes … yes he can. To make it stick on appeal, however, you will have to convince an arbitrator or other impartial adjudicator that the harm caused by just one or two incidents of misconduct warrants removal from government service. Removals based on only one or two incidents are affirmed all the time. However, they also are occasionally mitigated to a lower level of discipline because the reviewing judge decides that removal just isn't warranted based on the misconduct.

Take that risk if you must and the chances are decent that you will be sustained if the single incident of misconduct is serious. If you have the patience and perseverance, following the four-step Quick Start will avoid you having to convince some third party that the misconduct is serious enough to warrant a first-offense-termination because the very pattern of misconduct itself warrants removal regardless of what the actual harm to the agency might be.

See the Appendix for a collection of sample documents to implement a misconduct termination.

As for employees who engage in unacceptable performance rather than misconduct, a Quick Start guide would look just like a full-service guide as performance actions are extremely expedient and efficient, if you know what you are doing. You will know what you are doing by the time you finish that chapter later in this book.

Now that you know the basic approach to misconduct, the next chapters will give you the procedural and philosophical details and some recommended strategies for dealing with a variety of complicated situations.

CHAPTER 1
GETTING STARTED

If just showing up is half the battle, the other half is getting started. In this chapter, we will take you through the steps you should consider in the order in which you should consider them when first coming to realize that you have a problem civil servant on your hands.

Try Everything Else First

Although this is a book on how to fire employees who do bad things, we hope that you will never have to fire anyone. That is because the removal of a career government employee takes time, resources, and emotional involvement that would be better spent on other endeavors. When you fire someone, you adversely affect his employability perhaps for the rest of his life, plus you have to go through the trouble and expense of hiring a replacement. That's why we say we hope you never have to fire anybody. So, before you start the disciplinary process in earnest, we suggest that you try everything else first. It is easier on you and perhaps you will be able to convert an unacceptable employee into an employee who is at least doing a minimally adequate job. Of course, some misconduct or poor performance is so bad that a single incident warrants immediate termination. The guy who leaves the door open to the safe with all the secret documents and highly explosive materials probably warrants a quick goodbye. For most situations, once you realize that you have a problem employee, you will want to consider one or more of the following options:

- **Coaching.** Periodic informal instruction and feedback given by you or a seasoned coworker (a mentor) may help a minimal performer improve without having to resort to formal procedures.

- **Counseling.** While coaching can work with poor performers, misconduct warrants a little more direct discussion between you and the miscreant. Tell him what he did wrong and that you want him to do it right.

- **Training.** Sometimes, low performance can be improved through formal classroom or online training. Although the government usually does not have an obligation to train its employees, a three-day course in computer maintenance that helps your information resources technician improve to a point where he is being productive is a trivial expense compared to having to fire him for poor performance. Sometimes just asking the employee what training would be helpful gives valuable insight.

- **Reassignment.** Every job is made up of three components: the employee, the supervisor, and the work itself. If the employee is not working satisfactorily on a particular assignment, perhaps reassigning him to a new supervisor and/or a new position description will allow him the opportunity to become productive.

Although we could spend many pages devoted to discussing these techniques, doing so would be beyond the purpose of this book. Our objective is to help you to know what to do when all of your best leadership skills are unsuccessful, and you have reached the point of asking yourself, "What do I do next?"

The answer as to what to do next requires that you ask yourself a series of questions:

Question One: What is the employment status of the problem employee (e.g., has the employee just barely begun working for the government or is he in for the long haul)?

Most government agencies have more than one category of worker. When confronted with a problem employee, the first thing to do is to determine the employee's status in order to establish what procedures and rights apply. Here are some typical categories of employment and how to handle a problem employee who falls into each category:

Probationer - Most organizations, both government and non-government, have a probationary period for new employees to observe the employee in the work setting and to make a final determination as to employability. During probation, it is easier to summarily terminate an employee for poor performance or misconduct without a lot of procedures and without a lot of proof.

In the private sector, probationary periods usually are measured in weeks or months. In the federal government, by comparison, the standard probationary period is one year from the first day of employment (two years in the Department of Defense). If your problem employee is a probationer, the most you will need to do is to give the employee a letter stating that you have decided to terminate him and give the effective date (usually at the close of business the day of the letter). Local policy will determine the exact wording and timing of the letter, but the bottom line is that this is a very simple process, at least compared to what you will encounter with a career employee.

There are three traps to avoid when terminating a probationary employee.

1. A federal probationary period is over at the end of the last scheduled work shift that precedes the one-year anniversary of initial employment. Removals are effective at midnight on the day stated in the notification letter. If today is the last day before the

one-year anniversary of initial employment, and the employee's shift is over at 4:30 this afternoon, your probationary termination letter dated today will be effective at midnight, several hours after the employee's probationary period is over. A probationary termination letter under these circumstances would be defective and set aside because the employee is entitled to the full notice and appeal rights of a career employee as of 4:31 PM. Either make the termination effective on a date prior to the last day of the probationary period, or set a specific time for the removal to be effective on the last day, a time that is earlier than the end of the shift.

2. As a general rule, an employee who occupies a position identified as "probationary" may still have rights to file an appeal with the US Merit Systems Protection Board if that employee has completed more than a year of current continuous employment with the government in any positions other than temporary positions limited to one year or less. Be careful of the "probationary" employee who has come to work for you directly from employment with another component of the government without any break in service. That person might well be entitled to the full protections of a non-probationary employee.

3. Employees in the federal civil service have a variety of ways that they can challenge a management action, that they can "push back" against their supervisor. For example, an employee can file a claim of civil rights discrimination regarding just about anything that a supervisor might do to him. When that happens, you will want to be ready to defend yourself, to prove that you have valid reasons for doing what you have done.

The law does not demand any proof for you to terminate an employee during probation. Because a terminated probationer can challenge you through the discrimination complaint process (or in some other manner), always have a legitimate, bona fide, business-related reason for the removal. At a minimum, write down, date, and sign your rationale for the termination, and store that piece of paper somewhere you can retrieve it if needed. Be as specific as possible about your reasons, with dates and witnesses, if relevant. A statement that says, "I terminated John Doe because he turned in the Smith report a week late on September 9, 20XX" is much better than a statement that says, "Doe was always late with reports." Always have a bona fide reason for doing what you do.

As a side note, although it is permissible to reprimand or suspend a probationary employee (and a temporary employee) few agencies do. That's because if a probationary employee has engaged in misconduct that warrants any discipline, most managers would agree that it is better simply to remove and replace the employee rather than get involved in the complaints, grievances, and appeals that might result if you were to impose lesser discipline.

Supervisory probationer - In the federal government, first-time supervisors have to undergo a supervisory probationary period during which they are evaluated on their ability to supervise. If your problem employee is a supervisor within the first year of appointment to a supervisory position, you can demote the supervisor back to the last non-supervisory position held prior to promotion without having to use a lot of procedures or giving formal appeal rights. If the problem with the employee is misconduct or if it is not convenient for you to demote the employee to a non-supervisory position, then you can still use the full procedures for disciplining career employees that we will discuss later.

Temporary employee - Temporary employees can be terminated in much the same manner as probationers. It just takes a letter from the supervisor that says that the temporary appointment is being terminated effective on such-and-such date. But remember to have a bona fide reason articulated in your file so you can defend yourself if that becomes necessary.

Contractor - More and more people who work for the government work as contractors rather than as true civil servants. The termination of a contract employee is controlled by the provisions of the master contract between the government and the private sector company which is providing services through contract. Usually, it takes no more than a phone call from you to your contract manager in the procurement office to have that particular worker replaced. The exact process is individual for every contract, so check with your contracts office to find out the most expedient manner to get rid of the problem employee.

Political appointee - At the state and local government level, in some locations employees at all levels are considered "political" and serve at the will of the elected officials who are in charge of their organization. Such positions are often called "patronage" and are a holdover from the days when government jobs were handed out as favors to political supporters. The concept of a non-patronage civil service, invented, by the way, in China over 2,000 years ago, has replaced these political jobs in most larger jurisdictions, except for the top management positions in an administration.

Individuals who serve at the will of the President of the United States as political appointees may be summarily dismissed without notice, an opportunity to respond, or appeal rights. They can be told to leave, have their appointment terminated, and the only right they have is to retrieve their personal belongings from the worksite before you slam the door behind them as they exit the building. In fact, you can even mail their belongings to them if you cannot stand them in your sight anymore. You would not be reading this book if all federal employees were political.

Special appointment authorities – Most federal civil servants are appointed under the hiring authorities established by Congress under Title 5 of the United States Code. The rights and procedures for that group are the subject of this book. However, some federal employees are appointed using specialized unique appointment authorities; e.g., Title 38 health care professionals employed in the Department of Veterans Administration and a few other agencies, and Administrative Law Judges serving in a number of agencies throughout government. The procedures and options for dealing with those individuals are beyond the scope of this text, although their processes are often very similar to those described here for Title 5 employees.

Career employee - An individual who was hired as a federal employee from a competitive source (e.g., a regular government applicant) and who has completed a one-year probationary period (or the equivalent) is considered to be a career employee for the purpose of disciplinary rights. If you have ruled out each of the above employment categories and have determined that your problem employee is a career Title 5 employee, you must use the formal discipline and appeals procedures that make up the rest of this text.

Once you have determined that the status of your problem employee is career, then you will need to answer the next question:

Question Two: Is the employee's problem misconduct or poor performance (e.g., did the employee steal widgets or was he just really slow when he made them)?

For our purposes, all problem employees fall into one of three categories. Either their problem is poor performance, misconduct, or a combination of both. It is important that you decide early on which category fits your situation because the procedures and evidence requirements are different.

If the employee is breaking rules, he is engaging in misconduct. Rules can cover just about every aspect of the workplace: attendance, dress code, language, and even, in some situations, off-duty conduct. We will cover these procedures for you in detail in Chapter Two.

An employee has a performance problem if the problem you observe is described in the performance plan for his position. If he is not producing enough widgets, leaving too many typos in his work, or otherwise failing to meet a minimal level of performance set in his standards, you will probably use the unacceptable performance procedures described in Chapter Three to remove him from his position if he does not improve. Read the employee's performance plan. If the problem you have is related to any critical element(s) in the plan, you have a performance problem, not a misconduct problem. If the problem is not discussed in any critical element, then you have a misconduct problem by default.

A problem employee might be both engaging in misconduct and performing unacceptably. Technically, you can take a combined removal action based on both problems. However, these sorts of actions are legally challenging for the uninitiated. Most often, a supervisor will choose one or the other single basis and move forward from there.

Sometimes an incident of poor performance is so bad that exceptional measures are called for. One creative way to deal with an employee who is a poor performer is to convert what would otherwise be a typical performance action into a more expedient misconduct action, thereby saving time and effort. For example, say that one of an employee's annual performance standards reads something like this:

> *Critical Element No. One: Courtesy*
>
> *The employee shall treat customers of the agency with courtesy and respect, even in difficult situations.*
>
> *Outstanding: No instances of discourteous conduct toward an agency customer, and one or more unsolicited letters of appreciation from a customer.*
>
> *Exceptional: No instances of discourteous conduct toward an agency customer.*
>
> *Satisfactory: One or two instances of discourteous conduct toward an agency customer in any 90-day period.*
>
> *Minimally Acceptable: Three instances of discourteous conduct toward an agency customer in any 90-day period*
>
> *Unacceptable: More than three instances of discourteous conduct toward an agency customer in any 90-day period*

If an employee engages in four incidents of discourteous conduct toward an agency customer during any 90-day period of the rating year, you can rate him as Unacceptable and begin to take an unacceptable performance action. Alternatively, you could convert the problem into a disciplinary action by giving the employee an order to be courteous, and then initiating progressive discipline (see Chapter Two) when he disobeys the order. Or, if the act of discourtesy is very serious and you cannot take the chance of it being repeated, e.g., the employee cusses out the agency head, you are not bound to the performance procedures and may immediately propose a removal based on misconduct.

Question Three: Is the employee's position in a collective bargaining unit (e.g., is the position covered by a union contract)?

If the employee occupies a position legally defined as within a collective bargaining unit (e.g., a union), he is entitled to the protections and procedures provided for in the collective bargaining agreement (e.g., the union-management contract). If this is your case, you will need to consult early and frequently with your labor relations staff to make certain there are no special procedures with which you must be concerned.

Every collective bargaining agreement is unique and there are thousands of such agreements through government. In this text we focus on the basic requirements common to all government employees and leave you the responsibility to determine the specific constraints of any applicable union-management contact.

GUIDING PRINCIPLE

OK, now you have identified the status of your problem and the types of procedures you will need to use to deal with the problem, including terminating the employee. Before we take you to the specific procedures, however, we need to state the guiding principle that will control all of our advice and recommendations:

When it comes time to deal formally with a problem employee, do as little as possible, but as much as necessary.

Many government managers get bogged down or simply shy away from disciplining employees because of the procedural hurdles involved. One of the key ingredients making this whole exercise more palatable is to keep a low profile, act only when you need to act, and nail every procedural requirement as it comes up in the process. Think of yourself as a world-class bicyclist, holding back in the pack at the Tour de France to escape the head winds, and then pushing forward with all of your might when it comes time to prove what you can do.

As a government supervisor, the more actions you take, the more you expose yourself to criticism, complaints, charges, and head winds, and the harder it will be for you to be successful. Throughout this text, you will see that we recommend very short time frames, very concise (even sparse) documentation, and an emphasis on getting the process started and finished as quickly as is allowed by law. Remember, by the time you are here, you have tried everything else, and it has failed. Now is the time for Plan B, to remove the problem employee so you can bring in someone who is talented, proud, and happy to be a government employee.

- If your problem is an employee who is engaging in misconduct, who is not obeying the rules you have established for the workplace, go to Chapter Two.

- If your problem is an employee who is performing unacceptably, and you can identify at least one critical element the employee is failing, go to Chapter Three.

Trust the process.

Chapter 2
The Fundamental Elements Of Discipline

Management has the burden in every case of discipline of proving each element of its case by a preponderance (e.g., a majority) of the evidence. There are five fundamental elements in every misconduct case. They are not necessarily laid out in a particular format, like the format you will see neatly labeled below, but they must be present for discipline to be sustained on appeal. When you are thinking about your problem, consider each of these elements and be able to articulate what proof you would submit at hearing to prove each element.

Before we get into the five fundamental elements of discipline, there are a couple of things you need to know. First, the law of serious misconduct and performance actions in the executive branch comes from the decisions issued by an independent federal agency with world-wide oversight of almost all federal employees, the US Merit Systems Protection Board (MSPB or the Board). The Board is made up of three Presidential appointees who serve independent overlapping seven-year terms. All three cannot be from the same political party. The Board employs about 75 administrative judges throughout the country who conduct hearings and issue initial decisions in cases. Those initial decisions can be appealed by either the (former) employee or the (former employing) agency to the three Board members. The members vote on each case that is appealed, majority vote rules, and the Board's decisions are considered to be "stare decisis" controlling case law for all future personnel actions in government. Those final decisions subsequently can be appealed to the US Federal Circuit Court of Appeals, and from there even to the US Supreme Court. Final authority lies in the judicial system, although those courts tend to give deference in many areas to opinions of the Board.

Another concept you need in order to understand the five fundamental elements is the process of discipline. Reprimands are usually the lowest level of discipline in government, and almost always can be issued directly by the immediate supervisor. In other words, an employee's immediate supervisor has the authority to issue a reprimand – not human resources or the attorneys in the general counsel's office, just front-line management. Once you move above a reprimand to a suspension, demotion, or removal, when you're taking away the employee's money (or livelihood), in most every agency in government, two levels of supervision are required. The first level supervisor usually proposes the action and is known as the "proposing official." The second level (or higher) management official makes the decision regarding the proposal and is known as the "deciding official."

You will need to understand these terms and these procedures to fully appreciate the five elements of discipline below.

Element 1. You must prove you have a valid rule.

By definition, misconduct is a violation of a rule. Rules can come from many places in a government workplace. The most obvious source of rules is the law: the federal, state, and municipal statutes that govern the particular institution. For example, it is a federal law that a federal employee cannot misuse a government vehicle for personal reasons. Also, it is a law in the federal government that supervisors cannot discriminate against their employees based on race or sex. Rules that come from law are well-established, universal as far as their jurisdiction, and usually heavily litigated, thereby giving us a body of case law that helps us to understand what the law really means.

Rules can also come from individual government agencies or even local components of the agency. For example, the Internal Revenue Service (IRS) has an agency-wide rule that requires its employees to file personal tax returns in conformance with all the governing tax regulations. Employees at other government agencies are compelled by state and federal law to file their taxes properly, but the IRS has gone one step further to establish an administrative sanction for filing improperly. It is easy to see why the IRS has decided it is necessary to have an agency-specific rule in this area. We citizens are expected to comply with the tax code voluntarily. Some of us might decide not to do that if we knew that the very individuals responsible for monitoring our compliance with the code are code-breakers themselves. Agencies throughout government have agency-specific rules that apply just to their employees.

Local government facilities can also have rules: "No smoking within Building 123 or within 20 feet of any entrance or open window." "Employees are not to park in front of the emergency entrance." Local rules often are published in a policy manual or are sometimes simply posted as signs on the wall.

Most important, though, and perhaps the most misunderstood authority for a rule, is the individual government supervisor. Individual supervisors set rules every time they give an order, instruction, or set a policy for their particular workplace:

> *The policy in this office is that all employees are to check out with me before leaving for the day.*
> *Ed, I want you to close the door to your office before you engage in loud discussions on the phone.*
> *Turn off your computers before leaving work each day.*

Each of these is a statement a supervisor might make to establish a workplace rule, a rule that will result in discipline if the employee violates it. These rules are just as enforceable as rules passed by the U.S. Congress, implemented from upon high at agency headquarters, or published in a local policy manual. When an individual voluntarily accepts a position with a government agency, the implicit agreement within that employment relationship is that the employee will do what he is told in exchange for a government paycheck (or electronic deposit) every couple of weeks or so. If the employee does not want to do what he is told, that's just fine; he can go work somewhere else. If he wants to remain a civil servant, he has to obey his supervisor's direction just as he would obey a state or federal law, or go find himself another job.

Whoa! What a ground-breaking concept! Are we saying that an employee cannot refuse an order because the assignment is not one that is in the employee's position description? That a supervisor can order an employee to do just about anything and the employee has to obey? That if he doesn't obey, he can be disciplined? Are we REALLY saying that a supervisor does not need specific superior authority (e.g., a law, regulation, or published policy) before he can establish a rule for the employees he supervises?

Yes, as crazy as that might sound, that is EXACTLY what we are saying. In the game of government employment, the supervisor gets to decide what has to be done and the employees who report to that supervisor have to do it. Failure to obey a supervisor's order is just as clearly bad conduct as failure to obey a law of Congress.

Suppose an employee who works for you dresses in a very revealing manner; six-inch stiletto heels, super-short skirt, low-cut see-through blouse, midriff exposed from way below the belly button to the bottom of a short tight tube-top, and huge dangling earrings that look and operate more like a wind chime than jewelry. Customers to the agency have made comments, coworkers have complained, and frankly you yourself have been distracted more than you care to think about. Do you need an act of Congress to be able to get the employee to dress more conservatively? Do you need a published dress code that applies to all employees and in detail defines proper business attire? No, you need only your inherent authority as a supervisor to say to the employee:

> *Pat, don't dress like that anymore. It's too revealing and distracting to the people in the office. Dress more conservatively, as do Terry and Alex. If you have any questions about the appropriateness of specific items of clothing, talk with me.*

What, you say? Do we mean that government employees cannot wear whatever they want to work? Yes, that's right. Government employees have no basic right to dress any way that they want even if the agency they work for does not have a written dress code. The unwritten dress code throughout government is that an employee must dress in a manner that is appropriate for the work being assigned. And guess who gets to decide what is appropriate … yep, it is that employee's supervisor.

Of course, as a practical matter, it is a question of what the supervisor and the next level supervisor think is appropriate. That's because every employee has a right to grieve and grievances go up the chain of command. However, if a first-level supervisor can explain his business rationale for the order, in most organizations the upper levels of supervision should support that order.

What if there is a union? Unionized employees have the right to require management to notify the union and to bargain over changes to their "working conditions." There are several complex exceptions to this right that can allow management to make changes that do not constitute "negotiable" working conditions. If you supervise unionized employees, it is a good idea to run your planned instructions past your labor relations adviser before implementing any changes that may affect working conditions.

When you do this, keep two things in mind. First, even though legally you may be entitled to make a workplace change that does not need to be negotiated, your labor relations adviser may recommend that you notify and bargain with the union anyway. That is because front line labor relations is half legal, half relationship, and the other half is just plain luck (to paraphrase Yogi Berra). Sometimes it is best for the overall relationship to bargain workplace changes to avoid getting into a protracted legalistic fight with the union as to whether you need to bargain at all. The agency's labor relations specialist is in the best position to make this judgment.

Second, as much as we hate to say it, there are a few management advisers in government who have developed a posture over the years of just saying "no" whenever a supervisor proposes to make a change. Be aware of this tendency in a few people and push hard when you have things you want to do to make the workforce more efficient and effective. Many times, there is a "work around" that will allow you to do what you want to do; you just need a creative aggressive specialist in the field to help you figure out how to do it and to support you when you do. Be polite, but keep talking to people to see if anyone can think of a way to let you do what you need to do to improve your organization. If it does not make sense to you when you are advised you cannot do something, the chances are good that the law backs you up.

What if only one employee is causing the problem; can the supervisor give an order to just that person? This is one of the most misunderstood areas of a supervisor's authority, and perhaps made even more confusing because of those "just-say-no" advisers mentioned above. Consider this scenario:

> *Supervisor Smith has six employees who report to him. Each works in a private office and each uses the phone on occasion to conduct the government's business. When Smith walks around the office, he notices that Employee Edwards is on the phone almost constantly while the other employees are on the phone perhaps two to three times per day for no more than 10 minutes each call.*
>
> *Smith decides that he wants to give an order to Edwards that he keep a daily phone log of all calls with times, names, and subjects, and that the log be emailed to Smith at the end of every shift. Smith decides to run the question past his advisers for approval prior to implementing. What will the advisers tell him?*

Unfortunately, some advisers in this scenario will advise Smith that if he wants Edwards to keep a daily phone log, the five other employees must also be required to do the same thing. "Government employees are entitled to equal treatment, you know." Smith realizes that if he puts a similar requirement on his other good employees, the result will be a decrease in their efficiency and morale, so he decides to let Edwards slide.

Supervisors who believe (or are advised) that they must treat all employees the same are mistaken. Government managers must treat all employees FAIRLY, but that does not mean that they must all be given the same orders or have the same rules. Brace yourself for this because you will have to think about it for a minute:

Government supervisors are required by law to discriminate.

No, not to discriminate based on race, sex, age, disability, color, national origin, religion, genetics, veterans' status, whistleblower status, union activity, or any of the other "protected" categories of employee rights. Government supervisors are paid to discriminate among their employees based on MERIT; on conduct and performance. In the scenario above where Smith wants to give a person-specific order to Edwards, he is not only allowed to do that, he is encouraged to do it by law. Any advice to the contrary is simply misplaced.

When Smith gives a unique order to Edwards, can Edwards file a discrimination complaint? Of course. Can he file a claim of whistleblower reprisal, union retaliation, or a grievance? Absolutely. Employees are free to raise issues about fair treatment in several different forums. Nothing can stop them. Supervisors who are hesitant to give orders because they are afraid about having "charges" filed or being "sued" may very well decide not to require Edwards to keep a log. Of course, by doing so they are accepting performance and conduct that is inconsistent with an efficient work place. If that is the sort of supervisor you are, more willing to avoid conflict than to do the right thing, then we cannot help you much with this text. Part of the price we pay for a fair government is the right of government employees to have avenues of redress to protect them from unfair treatment. Part of the responsibility of being a government supervisor is to manage the workplace efficiently while simultaneously acknowledging the employee's right to challenge what he believes to be unfair treatment. A supervisor who is afraid to act because of the fear of an employee exercising a right of redress is not going to be very effective. Even though giving an order can open up a supervisor to a charge of unfair treatment, the order still needs to be given if workplace effectiveness is to be attained. And as long as the supervisor has a bona fide reason for taking whatever action he is taking, any discrimination charge/complaint/suit will fail.

Off-duty Misconduct. Can the supervisor establish rules for off-duty misconduct? Sometimes government employees break the law or violate agency rules when they are in an off-duty situation, in the evening after a tour of duty is completed or over the weekend or during a period of leave. Agencies sometimes feel a need to discipline employees for conduct that occurs away from the government workplace.

The fundamental principle that guides employee discipline in the federal service flows from the Lloyd-Lafollette Act of 1912. In that dandy little piece of legislation, Congress for the first time stated clearly that a federal employee can be terminated only for "such cause as will promote the efficiency of the service." In lay terms, that simply means that a federal employee can be disciplined only for job-related reasons, that there must be a nexus (a relationship) between the misconduct and the employee's federal position.

If misconduct occurs on the job during work hours, the nexus is almost indisputable. You will hardly ever have to be concerned about establishing a nexus for on-the-clock misconduct. That's because at a minimum, there is a misuse of government time and property.

If the misconduct occurs after hours, you will want to be very concerned about proving a nexus. That is because we as a society are hesitant to hold government employees accountable for actions that occur away from work when they are not being paid unless there is a clear connection between the misconduct and the interest of the government.

Agencies sometimes have formal rules targeted specifically to off-duty misconduct. Law enforcement agencies may have rules that prohibit law enforcement officials from engaging in social relationships with convicted felons. An agency financial department may have a rule that the comptroller and other senior financial employees cannot engage in outside business transactions that are based in fraud. All agencies may be able to discipline employees who bring disrespect on the government by engaging in notorious and egregious criminal activity. In each of these situations, the agency that takes discipline will want to explain to the reviewing administrative body why the rule is essential to the "efficiency of the service" and was thereby an appropriate intrusion into the employee's nonpaid life.

Consider this scenario:

> *You pick up your morning paper one day and see an article that says that one of your employees, a non-supervisory engineer who works one level below you in the organization, has pleaded guilty to a criminal charge of producing pornographic material depicting children. In exchange for his guilty plea, he will serve no jail time.*

When you arrive at work, you have an email waiting for you from the regional director who also read the article, and she wants to know what you are going to do about this terrible situation. Being a smart second-level manager, you figure that means discipline for the employee, so you start to look for a nexus to relate this off-duty misconduct to the work of the government. Here are some things you might look for:

- Did the employee use government equipment (email, copy machine, web access) in the furtherance of his criminal activity?
- Does the employee come into contact with children as a result of his government employment (nearby day care center, as an engineer he performs work in housing projects containing children, or perhaps he comes in contact with summer-hire high school or college students who are legally "children" because of their age)?
- Are the employee's coworkers aware of his crime and hesitant to work with him?
- Has the supervisor lost faith in his ability to trust the employee because he committed such a heinous crime?

- Is the public aware of the employee's criminal behavior and his position as a government employee, thereby bringing disrespect onto the agency?

The courts have held that certain types of crimes are so egregious that there is a "presumed nexus" thereby relieving the agency from having to prove the necessary relationship. The production of pornographic material depicting children just might reach that level. However, do not rely on untested theories if you can avoid it. Be ready to prove a nexus even if you think that the courts might find one presumed.

Is the fact that the employee was found guilty of committing a crime enough to warrant his removal from government service? No, it is not. As crazy as it might seem, conviction for committing a crime is not automatic grounds to fire a government employee. The supervisor still must relate the misconduct that constituted the crime to the employee's government position. Consider this hypothetical:

> *It is a federal crime to conspire to kill a bald eagle. One of your employees while off-duty conspires to commit this terrible crime and is sentenced to a year of probation. Can you discipline this employee?*

Well, like all good legal questions, the answer to this one is, "it depends." If the employee is a GS-2 file clerk deep in the bowels of the Department of Veterans Affairs, probably not. It would be difficult to relate the work of a low-level file clerk in an agency dedicated to providing services to our country's veterans to the crime of bald-eagle-killing-conspiracy. If the employee works for the U.S. Forest Service as a Range Manager and is responsible for overseeing the protection of endangered species such as the bald eagle, discipline including termination would easily survive a challenge to the nexus requirement. The lesson here is to look beyond the label "crime" and consider the misconduct itself. Does it harm the efficiency of the government because the employee engaged in this misconduct? If the answer is "yes" and you can prove that "yes" by a preponderance of the evidence, you can discipline the employee just as if the misconduct had occurred on the job.

Element 2. You must prove the employee had knowledge of the rule.

So now you have the rule firmly established. You worked through the union, you cleared everything with your supervisor and your advisers, and you are ready for the next step. A rule does you no good unless the employee knows about it. You must prove that the employee knew the rule before you can discipline him for breaking it.

Mens Rea: There are two legal concepts that come together to establish this element. First, there is a principle that comes from the criminal law side of our society that says before an individual can be found guilty of a serious crime, it must be shown that he had a mens rea, a Latin term for a "guilty mind," criminal knowledge or wrongful purpose. A person who shoots and kills someone when he accidentally activates an unknown booby trap by opening his front door will not be found guilty of any crime even though his actions resulted in the unjustified death of someone. That is because he lacked a mens rea relative to killing anyone. He was just opening his front door. Of course, the person who set the booby trap will most likely be found guilty of murder; his was the guilty mind in this scenario even though someone else pulled the trigger.

In much more mundane situations, you can see where lack of a mens rea can result in there being no misconduct to punish. An individual cannot be found guilty of parking in a no-parking zone if the sign is missing and there was no other way to know that the zone was restricted. A penalty cannot be enforced for the late-filing of a tax document if the taxing agency mistakenly gave the wrong date to the filer. Throughout our society, we require knowledge of the rule before we enforce punishment for misconduct.

Prior Knowledge: Second, the U.S. Supreme Court has found prior knowledge to be a requirement of the Constitutional principle of due process. We cover due process in more detail in a later section. Suffice it for our purposes here to say that knowledge of the rule prior to punishment for breaking the rule is an important legal principle throughout our society.

So how do you prove the employee knew the rule you have so carefully crafted or chosen? Well, you can point to the book that contains all the agency's policies and show that it's in there. But can you prove that the employee read the policies? If not, can you show that the employee had an obligation to (e.g. was directed to) read the policies, or that he attended training in which the policies were taught? Maybe the rule was posted on the agency bulletin board or can be found on the agency's web site. Unless you can prove that the employee checked those sources or had an obligation to and did not, you probably will not be able to establish rule knowledge.

You can tell an employee a rule, "Hey, Ed, wash out that coffee cup instead of leaving it dirty in the sink." However, does the employee know from this oral rule-setting that you mean he is to wash out his cup every time? How about if he leaves it dirty sitting next to the sink rather than in it; does that violate the rule? Be aware that you are perfectly within your rights to discipline an employee who violates a rule you have communicated orally. Be aware, however, that the employee might be able to successfully defend himself if he can show that your oral communication was vague or that he simply did not hear or accurately understand what your rule happens to be. There are three better ways than oral communication to establish that an employee has knowledge of a rule before you take discipline:

A. **Give him a letter** - Write your rule down, address the memo to the employee, and nail it on the door to his cubicle. OK, maybe don't nail it to the door, but deliver it in such a manner that it cannot be disputed he got it: hand it to him and make a note for the file the date you did so. This is a heavy-handed old-school way of establishing rule knowledge, but it works.

B. **Send him an email** - Use technology to your advantage. All you are trying to do at this stage is to get across to the employee what standard of conduct you expect. You can draft a nice formal memo on raised-ink letterhead as described above. Or, you can obtain the same tactical advantage with a simple email and cause much less consternation in the employee than would occur with the delivery of a big formal letter.

In fact, those supervisors who like a belt plus suspenders, and who like to make their legal counsel who must defend them VERY happy, just might employ the three-step shuffle below:

1. Tell the employee orally what the rule is: "Ed, I want you to keep a phone log, yada, yada, yada ...."

2. Then, as soon as you get back to your desk, send old Ed an email: "Ed, this is just to confirm our discussion of earlier this morning relative to a phone log ...." Lay it out in detail as to what you expect; what your rule is relative to Ed's maintaining a phone log. Your friends in information technology will now be able to show when you sent the email and when Ed opened it; good proof to have.

3. Finally, the next time you see Ed in the hall, "Hey, Ed, did you get my email about the phone log? Any questions?"

Keep contemporaneous notes of each discussion and your email, and you are well on your way to being able to establish Element Two without any problem.

C. **Progressive Discipline** - Sometimes a supervisor will discipline an employee at a low level, perhaps by issuing a Reprimand, when it is questionable just how clearly an employee was on notice of the rule. Yes, the supervisor told the employee not to take more than 30 minutes for lunch, but the employee did not really understand that he would be disciplined for an infraction of just a two- or three-minute deviation from the rule. A Reprimand would probably still stand in this situation if grieved, but more importantly, the NEXT time the employee comes back from lunch five minutes late, the fact that he has been disciplined previously for the same misconduct removes any argument that the supervisor's rule was equivocal. Knowledge of a rule sometimes is shades of gray more than a black-white question. With a Reprimand in the record, the supervisor gets rid of any alleged grayness and firmly establishes employee knowledge.

Does the supervisor always have to explicitly tell the employee the rule before taking discipline? Fortunately, no. You might remember one of the first principles of law you probably heard when growing up, "Ignorance of the law is no excuse." School kids just love to throw that phrase around trying to impress friends and scare the pants off of some playmate that happened to do something arguably improper. Yes, everybody thinks they ought to be a judge when they are in junior high school.

Ignorance of the law actually can be a valid excuse in some situations, especially when it comes to the level of penalty that will be imposed (see the discussion of the Douglas Factors later in this chapter) as well as in situations like the long lunch scenario discussed above. The best way to think of this is that you satisfy the employee knowledge requirement of Element Two if you can prove either the agency specifically informed the employee of the rule and thereby knew the rule, or the employee should have known the rule. You may not have a rule that says that an employee may not set fire to his supervisor's desk, but you can certainly terminate an employee who does. Here's a hypothetical to help you see where the line may be in these sorts of should-have-known situations:

> *The regional director asks the regional attorney to take on a special task. The new head of the agency is making an on-site visit tomorrow, and the director tells the attorney that it is his job to show the agency head around the facility, introduce her to all the department heads, and generally act as her escort for the day.*
>
> ***Scenario One:*** *The attorney reports for the assigned task the following day dressed in six-inch stiletto open-toed shoes, a very short mini-skirt, fishnet stockings, no shirt, body piercings and tattoos all over his torso, and wearing a hat bearing regulation-size antlers and colorful blinking LED lights.*
>
> ***Scenario Two:*** *The attorney reports for the assigned task the following day wearing black trousers, dress shoes, a white dress shirt with a black bow tie, and a bright plaid sport coat.*

The attorney in the first scenario can be disciplined. The agency does not need a specific rule that says an employee cannot wear antlers with blinking lights in the workplace. Common knowledge as to the acceptable dress of a professional employee given this work assignment would establish that the employee "should have known" the rule. Easy discipline case.

The attorney in the second scenario probably cannot be disciplined. Even if the immediate supervisor cannot stand bow ties and finds bright plaid sport coats to be the height of bad taste, it would be very difficult to prove that the employee should have known this to be unacceptable dress. If the supervisor in the second scenario sends an email to the employee telling him not to wear a bow tie or plaid sport coat in that situation, then we have an enforceable rule for which the employee can be held accountable if he breaks the rule in the future.

The bottom line to all of this is that you can discipline an employee based on common knowledge rather than specific notification, but you are more likely to be successful in cases in which the deviation from the common knowledge rule is significant and clearly harmful to the agency's interest.

Element 3. You must prove the employee broke the rule.

Technically, this is the easiest element to prove, and often it is the only element that an untrained supervisor may think is important. Now that you are deep into this text, you have an appreciation for the fact that this is just one element of five on which you have the burden of proof.

There are several ways you can prove the employee broke the rule. You may have a security video or other information retained by the agency's security system that shows that the employee did the bad deed or at least was present on the date that the deed was done. Today, computer programs can be used by an agency to track individual use of agency computers, particularly access to the web. As agencies often have rules about computer use, such programs can create strong proof of an employee's activities.

One of the most common methods of proof that the employee broke the rule is the statements of witnesses to the misconduct. Although eyewitness accounts are notoriously inaccurate (at least they are according to legal publications), they still are some of the best and most common evidence you can muster to support your burden of proof as to Element Three. Be wary of four traps that can occur when using witness statements:

1. The strongest evidence of a witness's account is the live testimony of that witness at hearing. That is because at hearing a witness will be subjected to cross-examination that will test the witness's ability to perceive, remember, and to testify free of bias. You can use written witness statements, but they are not as powerful; the sworn written statement of a witness that says, "Yes, Ed did it," is not going to carry the day if Ed takes the stand and swears under oath that, no, he did not. Live sworn testimony trumps cold written statements every time (all other things being equal).

2. If you must use written statements instead of live testimony, at least get the statement in affidavit form with a statement at the bottom that says that the signer understands he is required by law to tell the truth and that he attests under penalty of perjury that he is. Better yet, videotape the witness giving the statement. In any case, statements from witnesses about an act of misconduct must identify who the witness is. An agency cannot rely on a statement from an anonymous source to take discipline against an employee.

3. Sometimes coworkers who are witnesses to the misconduct will refuse to give statements to the supervisor investigating the incident because they do not want "to get involved." Well, they do not have a choice. If you direct coworker witnesses to give a written statement or to testify at hearing, they have to obey your order (i.e., your rule) or be subject to discipline themselves for insubordination. Even if they try to claim the Fifth Amendment protection from self-incrimination, there are ways you can work around that with the help of a good legal adviser.

4. Sometimes an incident of misconduct will involve only two witnesses: the perpetrator of the act and the victim. Often this is referred to as a he-said/she-said situation, and some supervisors

> believe that they cannot take discipline in this situation because they cannot prove who is telling the truth. Fortunately, that is not the case. If you discipline an employee for misconduct observed only by himself and the victim, the judge who hears the appeal will decide who is telling the truth when the two opposing versions of events come out in testimony. It cannot be easy for a judge in that situation because he is expected to be aware of inflections in voice, telltale body movements, and perhaps even beads of sweat. However, that is the responsibility he has and why he makes the big bucks in government service. If your only cooperating witness is the victim, do not be afraid to move forward with discipline if you conclude that the victim is being truthful. Ask your adviser to explain how to use the "Hillen Factors" to evaluate witness credibility.

We have talked a lot about proof and having enough proof to establish the five elements necessary for each case of discipline. But just how much proof is enough? Well, in most cases, surprisingly less than you might think. In the chart that follows, think of the numbers on the left of the vertical axis as relative estimates of the minimum amount of evidence necessary to prove a particular sort of "charge." In concept, these numbers are very similar to percentages. So for example, we know by law that for an agency to be successful in a disciplinary case, normally it must prove each element of its case by a "preponderance" of the evidence; e.g., the scales of justice have to be just barely tipping in favor of the agency; it is more likely than not that the agency's view of events is actually what happened. Compare this to an unacceptable performance removal. By law in the federal government an agency needs to submit only "substantial" evidence to support its action. Congress made this distinction to make it easier for agencies to build cases in the often-subjective area of performance appraisal. That is why in most cases it is easier for an agency to fire employees for poor performance as compared to firing them for misconduct.

In the Prologue, we described how Congress has changed the law that applies to firing most employees at the VA. One of the major changes is the lowering of the burden of proof in misconduct removals. Rather than needing a preponderance of evidence to fire a misbehaving VA employee covered by the new law, the supervisor needs to produce evidence only at the lower substantial level.

Now compare both of these actions to the level of proof necessary in heightened scrutiny situations. In the federal government, this standard comes into effect when an agency is disciplining a whistleblower or engaging in certain actions relative to employees with disabilities. Congress believes that these situations are especially subject to agency abuse and that greater employee protections are called for in the way of an increased burden of proof. If you are dealing with a federal employee who is a whistleblower, and you are preparing to fire that employee for unacceptable performance or misconduct, you will need extra proof to be successful even in the absence of any proof you are intentionally reprising against the employee (see Chapter Six for a more detailed discussion).

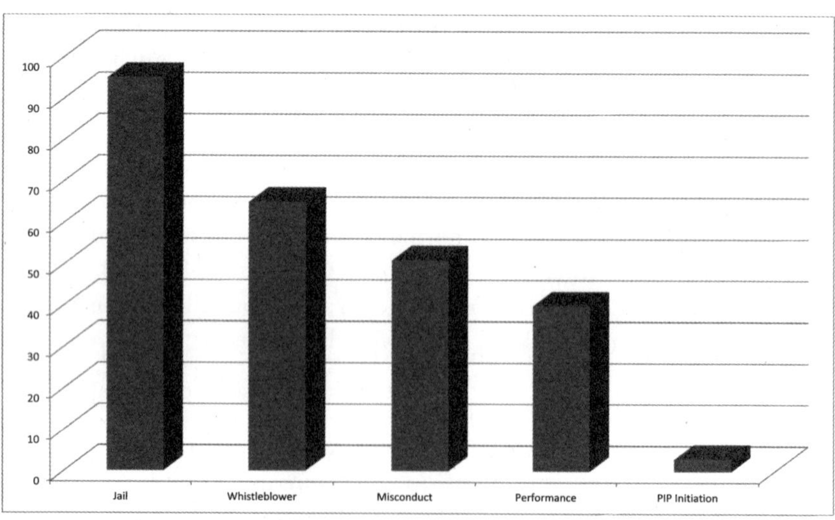

When you develop a case against an employee, do not be overwhelmed by the mistaken belief that you need to prove "guilt" at the same level as you would if you were prosecuting a criminal. You will have to prove the charged misconduct occurred, but only by the slightest majority of the evidence.

Element 4. You must prove your selection of penalty is reasonable.

It is easy to forget that the supervisor has to prove that the discipline level he selected is appropriate. Sometimes by the time you get to this point, you feel just great that you have a good rule in place and clear video of the employee breaking that rule, and are exhausted by the whole process. Do not reduce your efforts just yet. We still have a way to go before this action is in the can.

In the early days of the federal Civil Service Reform Act of 1978, there was much discussion as to who should be deciding what penalty was appropriate once misconduct is established. Agency representatives argued that only the agency could properly assess the myriad factors involved in the harm caused by an act of misconduct, and that once a reviewing body or court concluded that the misconduct occurred, the agency's penalty determination should be unimpeachable. On the other side, federal union representatives argued that the agency should not be in the penalty business at all because of all the variables involved, and that an oversight agency like the brand spanking new U.S. Merit Systems Protection Board should select the appropriate penalty to ensure consistency across the Executive Branch. As is often the case in philosophical disagreements inside the Beltway, the courts came down somewhere in the middle.

The law today recognizes two important aspects of the penalty selection process:

1. The agency makes the penalty determination based on the mitigating and aggravating factors relevant to the situation.

2. The Board will affirm the agency's penalty selection as long as the agency proves it properly considered all the relevant factors, and the penalty is within the bounds of reasonableness.

The supervisor's concern at this point is to make sure that he actually considered, and that there is proof in the record he actually considered, all the aggravating and mitigating factors relevant to the case. Those factors are known collectively as the Douglas Factors based on the lead case issued in 1981 establishing this principle. In *Douglas v. VA*, 5 MSPB 313 (1981), the MSPB enumerated a dozen potential factors that might be present in a case of discipline and which every supervisor should review prior to proposing or deciding a formal disciplinary action.

The Douglas Factors are:

1. The nature and seriousness of the offense and its relation to the employee's duties, position, and responsibilities, including whether the offense was intentional or technical or inadvertent, or was committed maliciously or for gain, or was frequently repeated.

2. The employee's job level and type of employment, including supervisory or fiduciary role, contacts with the public, and prominence of the position.

3. The employee's past disciplinary record. [Be sure not to include anything in the discussion of this factor that is NOT discipline; e.g., counseling, warning, etc. Mention only Reprimands and Suspensions in most cases].

4. The employee's past work record, including length of service, performance on the job, ability to get along with coworkers, and dependability. [The length of service discussion must include recognition of three separate periods: service with the employing agency, service with other Executive Branch agencies, and military service.]

5. The effect of the offense upon the employee's ability to perform at a satisfactory level and its effect upon the supervisor's confidence in the employee's ability to perform assigned duties.

6. Consistency of the penalty with those imposed upon other employees for the same or similar offenses. [Rely on your own personal knowledge of penalties imposed on other employees. You have no obligation to investigate what other discipline has been used by other supervisors.]

7. Consistency of the penalty with applicable agency table of penalties.

8. The notoriety of the offense or its impact upon the reputation of the agency.

9. The clarity with which the employee was put on notice of any rules that were violated in committing the offense or had been warned about the offense in question.

10. The potential for the employee's rehabilitation. [Look for apologies and other indicators that the employee is accepting responsibility for his actions.]

11. Mitigating circumstances surrounding the offense such as unusual job tensions, personality problems, mental impairment, harassment, or bad faith, malice, or provocation on the part of others involved in the matter. [The main one here is whether there is an underlying medical condition causing the misconduct.]

12. The adequacy and effectiveness of alternative sanctions to deter such conduct in the future by the employee or others.

And, any other relevant aggravating or mitigating factors.

Note the last catch-all phrase above following the twelve primary Douglas factors. That means that if there are any factors that weigh for or against a penalty, the proposing and deciding officials should consider them even if they are not specifically enumerated in Douglas. For example, the Board has held that an arrogant attitude exhibited by an employee during an oral response can fairly be considered by the agency as an aggravating factor when selecting an appropriate penalty. If it affects the supervisor's penalty selection decision, it should be included in the Douglas Factor analysis.

A good human resources office will provide the supervisors involved in a disciplinary action with a worksheet to document adequate consideration of the relevant Douglas Factors. Failure to properly consider even one relevant factor can result in the Board stepping in and substituting its judgment for the agency's as to the maximum reasonable penalty. If that happens, the Board may mitigate the discipline selected by the agency and direct that a lesser penalty be imposed. In practice, this often means that the agency's removal will be set aside and a suspension or demotion put in its place. So be sure that you consider all the relevant Douglas Factors, listen for any mitigating factors raised by the employee in his defense of his actions, and then consider them, too. If you do, then the Board and the courts will be hesitant to step into the shoes of agency management and select a different penalty.

As a practical matter, the silver bullet in penalty selection is, if possible, to use progressive discipline. First offense removals (e.g., removals in which there is no prior discipline) receive close scrutiny from the Board because of the potential for unfairness or over-reaction. On the other hand, a case that is appealed in which the employee first received a Letter of Reprimand, then a 5-day Suspension, and for icing, a 14-day suspension all for the same misconduct within the agency's reckoning period (often two years), will almost never have a problem with penalty defense. A termination is not only reasonable, but probably called for in the case of an employee like this who simply cannot learn to obey rules. Even without the 14-day suspension, as is currently recommended by Government Accountability Office, the employee who commits three violations of the same rule within a relatively short period of time most likely warrants termination for the third offense, especially if the harm to the agency caused by the misconduct is significant.

Three thoughts about progressive discipline:

1. Do not be the supervisor who appears at the desk of the agency's employee relations specialist and demands to fire the employee who has been late returning from lunch by five minutes 100 days in a row, and is told he cannot do that. "What do you mean I can't fire someone who has been late 100 times? What kind of government bureaucracy is this?" Unfortunately, it is the kind of government bureaucracy that says that a supervisor is to start with lower levels of discipline to attempt to rehabilitate an employee before firing him. Don't fight the bureaucracy; learn what it requires and satisfy those requirements. When it comes to discipline, start early and

low, and increase your level of discipline until the employee either stops the misconduct or gets fired. A good mantra is, "Reprimand early, reprimand often."

2. Do not conclude that progressive discipline is mandatory. Serious misconduct should be dealt with seriously even if it is a first offense; "Well, Ed, I see that you have burned down the computer center, fired live ammunition at our customers, and parked illegally. As this is your first offense, I'll be giving you a Reprimand in the hope that you will mend your ways." The Board has held that Douglas Factor number one is the most important: the seriousness of the misconduct. If it's serious enough, remove him for a first offense. If in doubt, spend a little time reading the cases that were brought by other government supervisors (www.mspb.gov) and talking with your advisers. That will give you a valuable perspective on your situation.

3. Classic progressive discipline is: 1st offense, reprimand; 2nd offense, suspension; 3rd offense, removal. However, keep in mind that progressive discipline is not mandatory. A first offense may warrant removal if the harm is serious enough. Also, be aware that a Reprimand in Lieu of Suspension is a creative, flexible, expedient alternative to implementing a suspension for a second offense. The best way to implement a Reprimand in Lieu of a Suspension is to propose a suspension as you normally would for a second offense (or for a serious first offense). Then, after the employee responds and defends himself, offer the employee the option of his accepting a reprimand as an alternative to the proposed suspension. Condition the offer on the employee's acceptance of responsibility for his misconduct, understanding that the Reprimand in Lieu of a Suspension carries the same progressive discipline weight as would a suspension, and waiver of grievance/complaint rights to challenge the action. You will find an example of a Letter of Reprimand in Lieu of a Suspension in the appendix of this text, along with many other useful sample documents.

A Difficult Point Relative to Penalty Comparison

Douglas Factor 6 has always required that when selecting a penalty in a particular case, the deciding official had to consider penalties given out to similarly-situated employees within the same chain of command. That was the law of the land for nearly 30 years. Beginning in 2010, MSPB changed that requirement and began to require that deciding officials chose penalties no greater than penalties (or non-penalty outcomes) imposed by other managers throughout the agency, at least within the past three or four years. The three 2010 decisions that began this unfortunate shift came to be called "The Terrible Trilogy."

The previous edition of this textbook described The Terrible Trilogy as the most dangerous, destructive, bizarre approach the Board has ever taken with any issue of misconduct. It strikes at the very foundation of the civil service system, essentially mandating centralized decision-making within an agency, revoking the front-line managers' authority to manage organizational discipline, and resulting in more employees being fired than before. Yes, you read that correctly. This new approach to "comparator" employees forced agencies to keep the bar high and eschew both compromise and leniency in the name of agency-wide consistency. If a fellow supervisor in your agency has fired someone for misuse of a credit card, you will be forced to fire your employee who misuses his credit card, because if you don't, you have given reason for the prior removal to be set aside by MSPB.

As of this writing, there is good news and not-so-good news relative to this comparator-employee issue. Starting in 2014, the Board has slowly drifted away from the draconian comparator penalty approach of 2010 and subtly replaced it with the pre-2010 approach that focuses more on the discipline within a local chain of command rather than within the entire agency. In addition, by executive order the President has stated that penalties need not be consistent agency-wide to be valid penalties.

The not-so-good news is that this drift in Board law has not been clearly announced. In other words, there's no single decision out there yet that says, "Boy, oh boy, did we make a mistake back in 2010 when we issued the Terrible Trilogy." Instead, bit by bit, the members have begun to issue decisions that focus on differences between comparator employees.

Today, as best we can tell, management has no obligation to search for comparator employees. The proposing and deciding officials can make their respective decisions based on their personal knowledge of the penalty history within their organization. Employees have to raise the issue of comparator employees; the supervisor does not have to raise it for them. When trying to distinguish among employees relative to penalty selection (e.g., when trying to defend removing someone who did something similar to an employee who received lesser discipline), look to these areas of potential difference:

Different supervisors
Different organizational unit
Different deciding officials
Significant time between the penalties
Different types of positions
Different charged misconduct
The penalty imposed in the past was too lenient

In an ideal situation, the proposing and deciding officials will be able to honestly say something like, "I have never known of any other agency employees who engaged in similar misconduct under similar circumstances."

Element 5. You must prove the employee was provided due process.

Actually, the case law says that the agency is presumed to have provided due process unless the employee challenges that presumption. The better and more pro-active course of doing business is just to put this element on the agency's side of the burden of proof listing and make sure you can defend yourself if you are challenged.

Due process is a concept that comes from our Constitutional Bill of Rights: "No person shall be … deprived of life, liberty, or property without due process of law." In lay terms, that means that our government cannot take away the property of a citizen without using due process procedures. In a federal agency workplace, the supervisor is the government, the employee is the citizen, and the employee's job is the property. In a private sector company, there is no entitlement to due process in a disciplinary action because the Bill of Rights controls the government, not private enterprises. This is perhaps the most fundamental distinction between government and private sector employment.

Interestingly, the concept of due process is relatively limited. To provide due process prior to taking away a citizen's property, the government must tell the citizen why it is being taken, give the citizen an opportunity to argue why it should not, then consider the response in making its final decision. There is no Constitutional right to a hearing, to a lawyer, or to anything else other than notice, an opportunity to respond, and fair consideration. The good news for government supervisors is that the procedures for initiating discipline against an employee always provide minimal notice and due process. Sometimes the notice is 30 days; sometimes it is less. Sometimes the opportunity to respond is in writing, other times it may be oral (or both). Whatever the case, the Constitution is satisfied by the formal procedures employed in every government agency to remove problem employees.

Due Process: There are two areas, however, that can be a trap for the unwary supervisor even when the formal procedures are being followed. Do not make either of the following mistakes:

1. **Ex parte communications** - Here is another fancy legal-Latin phrase that attorneys just love to throw around to sound as if someone actually paid attention in law school. The term refers to a one-sided communication and rears its ugly head in the following hypothetical:

> Supervisor Smith proposes to Director Doolittle that Ed Edwards be fired for six days of Absence Without Leave (AWOL). During his oral reply, Ed tells the Director that he is being singled out for punishment by Smith and that other employees are AWOL without any punishment. Also, he tells the director that he has

> been having a lot of personal problems with his family that has caused his absences.
>
> Being the compassionate director that he has always thought he was, Doolittle calls Smith into the office, tells him he's thinking about reducing the penalty to a suspension, and asks Smith about Ed's claims. Smith not only denies any disparate treatment, but throws in that Ed steals other employees' food from the refrigerator, has not met any of his performance goals for the year, and that he smells bad four out of five days each week due to poor personal hygiene. Based on this additional information, Doolittle decides to impose the proposed removal.

This hypothetical demonstrates classic ex parte communication. Smith has given the deciding official information relative to Ed's conduct and performance in a manner that Ed cannot challenge because it is a one-sided communication; Ed is not aware of this new information that Dolittle has considered. If, on appeal, Ed can prove that an ex parte communication occurred, he will be restored to employment, especially if Doolittle admits he would not have imposed removal were it not for this additional information.

The agency can do two things to avoid this trap. First, once a disciplinary action is proposed, the proposing and deciding official should not discuss or communicate about anything regarding the case. There are exceptions to this general admonition, of course, and the case is not a guaranteed loser even if a substantive discussion occurs. It is simply a smart idea to limit your exposure and not have to explain any more than necessary when appearing before a judge. The primary policy should be for the deciding official to avoid making a final decision in the matter until the employee has had a chance to respond to the charges.

By the way, it is perfectly legal and probably a smart idea for the proposing and deciding officials to discuss the situation BEFORE the proposal letter is issued. It would be a common practice for a supervisor having a problem with an employee that might warrant removal to discuss the situation with his own supervisor, and the law does not prohibit those discussions.

Because the second-level manager may well become a deciding official in a proposed removal action, the deciding official has to be wary of two potential traps:

1. The senior manager must not pre-decide a penalty. It would be a violation of due process if the second-level supervisor were to say to the first-level supervisor, "Well, Sue, I think I've heard enough. Ed deserves to be fired for what you've told me, and I expect you to initiate that action very soon." A deciding official needs to hear the employee's response to the charges before making a decision. However, a deciding official does not violate due process by saying something like, "Well, Sue, I think I've heard enough. You need to move forward with your decision as to what to do about Ed."

2. When making his decision on a proposal, the deciding official absolutely must not consider any facts other than those facts in the proposal letter and those facts in the employee's response. We have seen cases recently that were reversed by the Board because the deciding official when selecting a penalty relied on his personal knowledge of the employee, conducted an independent investigation of the charges and the employee's defenses, and got advice from human resources about the effect the charged misconduct would have on the employee's security clearance. One agency was found to have violated due process when the deciding official Googled the name of the employee and found a bunch of stuff on the web that affected his penalty determination. When an agency violates due process, it automatically loses the case and the employee automatically gets his job back, with back pay and attorney fees.

Alternatively, if a Smith-Doolittle discussion occurs as described above, either by accident or because of the deciding official's sincere desire to investigate allegations made in the employee's response, the case can be rehabilitated by notifying the employee of these new allegations and allowing him the opportunity to respond. The easiest way to do this is for the deciding official to gather together all the new information and send it to the employee with a cover memo that says something like, "Because of issues you raised in your response to the proposed removal, I have conducted an additional investigation into your situation. The new information I gathered during that investigation is attached to this memo, and I intend to rely on it in making my decision. You have the next seven days to respond both orally and in writing to this information, if you choose. I will make my decision after your response or that time period passes without a response."

2. Improper charge framing - The supervisor frames the charge when drafting the proposed discipline letter. Framing a charge simply means describing the misconduct on which the supervisor is basing the proposed discipline, in a manner which allows the employee to defend himself. A charge that is framed improperly violates due process because the employee is not on notice of why the government is proposing to take his property, i.e., to fire him from his job.

For example, suppose that an employee's removal is proposed for "theft of a laptop." During his response before the deciding official, he convinces the deciding official that he did not intend to take the laptop and keep it permanently; he just wanted to borrow it for a few weeks so he could learn to play a new video game he had. The deciding official concludes that his intent was to return it after his game playing days were over, but the deciding official decides to take discipline anyway based on the employee's failure to gain approval to borrow the laptop for that purpose and for that length of time. If the employee appeals this decision, the discipline will be overturned based on improper charge framing. A "theft" charge requires the agency to prove the employee had the intent to permanently deprive the agency of the object taken. The deciding official disciplined the employee even though the record shows the employee did not have the requisite intent. Had the agency framed the charge as "unauthorized possession of a laptop" the discipline would be sustained.

This area of law has become very complicated over the years. In fact, it is so difficult to understand and apply that attorneys who work in this field often spend several days in legal seminars trying to understand what is required for an agency to satisfy its burden to provide due process by adequately framing a charge. For those supervisors with a good support team, this is not an area in which you need to get bogged down. Simply describe the misconduct to your support staff, and rely on them to craft a defensible charge that will pass muster on appeal. You have plenty to worry about without having to understand this unfortunately complicated area of discipline law.

Well, that covers the five fundamental elements that an agency must prove in every disciplinary action to be sustained on appeal. In some cases, some elements will be more challenging than others. However, every case has to have a check mark by every fundamental element or the discipline is likely to be reduced or reversed altogether on appeal.

We will cover a few of the more difficult discipline situations in later chapters. Right now, though, we want to move into the alternative basis for firing someone from government - unacceptable performance actions.

CHAPTER 3
UNACCEPTABLE PERFORMANCE REMOVALS

In the federal government, there are two separate and distinct procedures for dealing with a problem employee: conduct and performance. While management has the burden in a case of misconduct of proving each element by a PREPONDERANCE of the evidence, in an unacceptable performance case, the agency must prove each element only by SUBSTANTIAL evidence, a lesser burden of proof. Sadly, a recent MSPB study revealed that 93% of federal supervisors believed it took much more proof to remove an unacceptable employee. Congress specifically intended to make it easier for a supervisor to fire a federal employee for unacceptable performance as compared to misconduct when it established this lower burden of proof. In addition, Congress stated that it intended the appellate review of performance-based actions to be limited and less intrusive than in a case of misconduct.

Unfortunately, experience teaches that this intent of Congress expressed nearly 40 years ago has been defeated to an extent by the cumbersome procedures required to take a performance-based removal. The law can be read to allow for an expedited removal of a poor performer. However, the regulators and the courts have inadvertently made it difficult when an employee is not working up to standard for an action to be taken quickly. It has been said that the best thing that can happen to a supervisor who is confronted with a poor performer is for the employee to punch him out. At least the misconduct termination for striking a supervisor can be implemented relatively quickly.

In this chapter, we will give you suggestions for taking a performance-based removal as efficiently and fairly as possible. Remember, a major goal in any termination action is to do as little as possible and as much as necessary. That golden rule is especially important in a case of unacceptable performance because it is so easy for the procedures to get out of hand resulting in a slow ungainly march to nowhere, thereby giving the employee lots to complain about on appeal.

There are four fundamental elements in every unacceptable performance case. They are not necessarily laid out in a particular format, like the format you will see neatly labeled below. However, they must be present for a removal or demotion to be sustained on appeal. When you are thinking about your problem, consider each of these elements and be able to articulate what proof you would submit at hearing to prove each element.

Element 1. Write good standards.

Performance terminations that fail historically are reversed on appeal because of an improperly worded performance standard, not because of a failure of the agency to prove that performance was unacceptable. Let us rephrase that and repeat the point for emphasis:

Performance removals that fail usually fail because of improperly written standards.

We cannot overemphasize how important it is that the supervisor writes defensible standards that will withstand scrutiny on appeal. The twin keys to a good standard are objectivity and measurability. If you can reduce your job expectations for an employee to an objectively measurable indicator of some sort, you can defend your performance standard on appeal and most likely your action will be sustained.

In 2004, the law changed in this area to the great benefit of the federal manager. For nearly 20 years, the courts held that in addition to being objective and measurable, a standard usually must allow some margin of error. That principle resulted in the Board and courts setting aside performance-based removals if it was determined on appeal that the standards required perfect performance (e.g. an "absolute" standard such as, "Any typos in a document are unacceptable").

The rule of law that supported a bar on using an absolute standard has been reversed by the court and the Board, with the Board saying upon reconsideration of the issue, "An agency is free to set a standard as high as it thinks appropriate, so long as those standards are objective" and are related to the job. This is a significant change in the standard for reviewing performance standards and should result in even fewer removal actions being reversed on appeal. Theoretically, a supervisor could develop a standard that says removal is appropriate for a motor vehicle operator who drives one mile an hour beyond the speed limit on one occasion in a one-year period, or for a telephone operator who fails to answer one call out of thousands in more than one ring. Of course, there is no advantage for a supervisor to set a standard that is almost unattainable. It should be reassuring to know that you will no longer have to be concerned about proving to a third party that a production standard you have set is not absolute. Just be sure you can show your application of the standard, though high, is attainable.

Here are some standards that the Board has found to be improper:

> ***Employee Development Specialist, GS-12***
> ***Critical Element:*** *Develops and manages an effective training program.*
> ***Minimally Satisfactory:*** *Policies and procedures are unclear and fail to provide direction. Management of the program is inconsistent or poorly organized. Employees are not fully aware of training plans. Contacts are usually in the regional personnel office or OPM.*

MSPB found three critical errors in this standard. First, although it is labeled "minimally successful" it actually states "unacceptable" performance: "Policies and procedures are unclear and fail to provide direction." How does the employee rate below that standard? Perhaps, "Policies and procedures are really really unclear … ." An employee who performs at the minimal level can never be terminated from his position. By law, only unacceptable performance warrants removal. The first problem with this standard is that it should have been labeled "Unacceptable."

Second, the Board found this standard to be too subjective. For example, how do you measure whether program management is "inconsistent" or "poorly organized"? The law requires standards to be objective, and this one is not.

Finally, MSPB concluded that this standard simply was not measurable. "Contacts are usually in the regional personnel office or OPM." Even if the vague "usually" is changed to the more objective, "The majority of contacts are in the regional personnel office or OPM," how does a supervisor measure performance against such a standard? An employee development specialist may have 10 – 15 contacts a day. Does the supervisor stand in the corner with a clipboard and keep score of where those contacts are being made? Not only must the supervisor develop a method of measuring performance, the method must be explained to the employee. Without a realistic way of measuring performance, the standard would be unusable even if all the other problems were fixed.

Here's another loser standard:

> ***General Engineer, GS-11***
> ***Critical Element***: *Energy awareness.*
> ***Unacceptable Level:*** *Major assistance is required at least 50% of the time to complete articles for the energy awareness newsletter. Requires assistance at least 50% of the time when communicating in writing and when speaking formally.*

MSPB reversed the removal based on this standard because the Board decided that the way it was written required a higher performance rating as the requirement for assistance increased. In other words, if major assistance being required "at least" 50% of the time warrants an Unacceptable rating, requiring major assistance 80% of the time might warrant an outstanding rating plus a performance award. The Board firmly declared this to be an "unusable" standard, and held it to be invalid. Theoretically it would have upheld the standard if it had said something like, "Major assistance is required more than 50% of the time ..." although even then, there is a question as to whether the word "major" is overly vague.

Perhaps more importantly, though, the last sentence of this standard requires an Unacceptable rating to be given if the employee requires significant assistance when communicating "in writing and when speaking formally." Notice what the simple conjunctive "and" does to that standard. It requires that the employee fail BOTH as a writer AND as a speaker before an Unacceptable rating can be awarded. The incumbent could be the worst writer in the history of the government, yet just barely articulate enough to escape needing assistance when speaking more than 50% of the time, and he could not be terminated. Do not make life any harder on yourself than necessary. Use the conjunctive "or" in this situation and give yourself more flexibility when confronted with this situation.

Here is one last standard to consider. If you were a Board member, would you uphold a removal based on this language?

> ***Mechanic Foreman**, WS-8*
> ***Critical Element**: Maintains full knowledge of the shop and projects.*
> ***Satisfactory**: Normally familiar with most of the on-going work. Competent technical advice normally can be provided to subordinates to achieve an effective work product. In most cases, assures that work is completed on time according to the unit work plan.*

Smells pretty bad, doesn't it. Look at all those subjective words: "normally," "most," "effective work product." You would think that the Board would have no problem with reversing a removal based on this standard.

Well, believe it or not, the removal of this employee was upheld for the following reasons even though the standard is not very objective:

- This standard is for a supervisory position. The courts have held that because the nature of their work is very hard to measure, supervisors and professionals (doctors, lawyers, scientists, etc.) can be given relatively subjective standards.

- The supervisor of this position issued the employee at least two "fleshing out" letters prior to initiating the removal action that explained what the vague words really meant: "Your performance standard requires that you be normally familiar with most of the ongoing work in your organization. Last Thursday, I asked you about your progress on the XYZ project. You responded that you had never heard of the XYZ project even though I have personally sent you three emails and a preliminary report about the project. Etc., etc., etc."

As you can see, it can be a tricky assignment to craft a defensible performance standard. Given that every work situation is a little different from the next and that performance standards are often individualistic and unique, the best advice we can give you in our limited space in this text is:

> Draft the most objective standard you can.
> Run it by an employee relations expert to make sure it is defensible.
> At every stage in which you communicate with your problem employee, ask him if he has any problem understanding the standard and tell him what you expect him to be doing. Document his response and go the extra mile in explaining what you want.

If you do these three things, you will have a much better chance of defending your standard and succeeding in any termination or demotion action you take than would a supervisor who tries to go it alone without help or without an understanding of the potential pitfalls in standard writing.

Bonus: After all these years, we have finally developed a beautifully simple and powerful method of writing a whiz-bang legally terrific critical element. You may find that method in the appendix to this book.

Element 2. Implement the standards and measure performance.

Implementing a performance standard involves three aspects:

1. Employee participation in the development of the standard,
2. A reasonable period of time for the employee to get up to speed under the new standard, and
3. Your ongoing evaluation of the employee during and after the period of time he is getting up to speed.

Employee participation in developing the standard is required, but the amount of participation is completely within your control (unless your control is defined by language in a collective bargaining agreement). At a minimum, and what is common in many agencies, is that after the supervisor has drafted a set of standards, he will give them to the employee and allow the employee to recommend changes and make comments. The supervisor is free to reject any or all of the employee's recommendations or to implement some or all as he sees fit. Even though the employee gets to participate, the final decision as to the appropriate standards will belong to the supervisor.

Once the employee is given new standards, we know he must have a "reasonable" period of time to adjust to them and to demonstrate whether he can perform at an acceptable level. The concept of a "reasonable period" will vary from position to position and even employee to employee. It is safe to say that where an employee is on a standard 60 days or longer, he has been given more than a "reasonable period" to adjust. Remember, this requirement applies only when a new standard is introduced, for instance, when an employee moves into a new position or when a supervisor decides to implement a rewritten standard because of a change in work requirements. It does NOT apply when an employee simply moves from one performance year to another. Even though the employee may be given new standards at the beginning of an appraisal year, unless those standards differ in substance from the standards of the previous year, no adjustment period is necessary.

Finally, once the employee has standards and has been given a reasonable period of time to get adjusted, the supervisor needs to measure and evaluate performance periodically to determine whether the standards are being met. This evaluation probably will be informal at first, but may become more structured as unacceptable performance begins to rear its ugly head. Even then, however, the most the supervisor will have to document is most likely a note to file or an annotation in a notebook as to what was measured and on what date. Little documentation is called for at this stage because the next step is the first true step in dealing with a performance problem employee. From that point on, the documentation requirements will be intense.

Critical Semantics: Before we get into the procedural steps necessary to hold an employee accountable for poor performance, we need to clarify a highly important, often-misunderstood term.

When Congress passed the *Civil Service Reform Act of 1978*, it created a brand-new way to hold federal employees accountable for poor performance, 5 USC Section 4302. That law allowed for an agency to fire a poor performer, but only after the employee had been given a chance to demonstrate whether he could perform acceptably. OPM was empowered by that law to issue implementing regulations.

When OPM issued those regulations, it made a critical error. In 1981, in 5 CFR Part 432, it said that prior to firing a poor performer, the agency must initiate a "Performance Improvement Period" (subsequently renamed by OPM as the "Performance Improvement Plan"). That's where we got the acronym "PIP" and the concept that this was a time for the failing employee to "improve" his performance.

Well, an opportunity for improvement was never required by law. The Reform Act said that the agency could fire an unacceptable performer after giving the employee "an opportunity to demonstrate acceptable performance." 5 USC 4302(c)(6). There is a world of significant difference between a period to improve performance and a period to demonstrate performance.

Consider these two examples:

- **Demonstration:** You ask an individual to demonstrate whether he can play the piano. I would guess that it will not take you more than a minute or two to determine whether the individual can play more than a note.

- **Improvement**: You ask an individual to improve his piano playing. Well, his first attempt is horrible. But since improvement carries the concept of more than one attempt, his next session he is a little better. And by his third session, he has discovered that the black keys sound differently from the white keys. Maybe on his fourth or fifth session, he will discover those nice brass pedals at his feet. After several sessions, he's still a terrible piano player, but we have to admit, he has improved from day one. Even professional pianists admit that improvement is an ongoing process, sometimes lasting years to a lifetime.

Keep in mind that when an individual is hired into a government position, he has put forward credentials that support his contention that he can indeed perform acceptably in the position. Then, as we've noted previously, the law requires that a newly hired employee must be given a "warm-up" period of maybe 45-60 days to get used to the job. It makes perfect sense that an individual who has crossed these two hurdles who still isn't able to do his job does not need an "improvement" period. He should have a chance to "demonstrate" his skills or be moved onto something else.

Think of this pre-firing period as you would a final examination. You did not walk into a final exam in college and have the professor begin a lecture, to improve your knowledge of the material. No, you were tested and given an opportunity to demonstrate your mastery of the knowledge you were expected to possess after completing the course. That's what Congress always intended for this opportunity period to be; a chance to *demonstrate* knowledge and skills, not to *acquire* knowledge and skills.

Today, OPM's regulations have been corrected. They now direct that prior to firing a poor performer, an agency must give the employee "an opportunity to demonstrate acceptable performance." 5 CFR 432.104. At least one major agency has done away with the awkward and incorrect concept of a "PIP" and now refers to this period as an "ODAP." Other agencies call it an "Opportunity Period" while still others call it a "Demonstration Period." Unfortunately, the unique acronym PIP has been used so long it has developed an almost universal recognition factor.

In the most recent Executive Order to address this issue, the White House chose to abandon the concept of "improvement" in the naming of the period. Instead, the EO makes reference to demonstrating acceptable performance prior to removal. Still, we are left without a workable abbreviation.

It would be helpful if OPM would give us a nice acronym to use to replace the PIP abbreviation, one that embodies the demonstration concept found in law rather than emphasizing the incorrect concept of improvement. As it has not, we are left to our own devices to create a short-hand reference to the statutorily-required pre-firing period for poor performers. Given that anything with an "I" in it could be misinterpreted, and given that long abbreviations like "ODAP" are sort of awkward (sorry), for purposes of this text we've decide to call the old PIP a Demonstration Period or DP.

Yes, in our seminars and even in this textbook, we may slip occasionally and make reference to a PIP (.e.g., the evidence burden bar chart in the previous chapter). However, we will endeavor to use the abbreviation DP instead of PIP as it is a more accurate description of the obligation the supervisor has, and the opportunity the employee is guaranteed by law. Perhaps by the next edition of this text, OPM will have formalized an abbreviation for the use by all of us.

A Defensive Narrative: Flip back to the bar chart in the previous chapter, the one that compared the burdens of proof necessary for different categories of government action. Notice that the lowest burden of all is at the far right, the amount of proof necessary to implement a DP (a PIP). The law doesn't even have a name for this level as it is almost nonexistent. However, because of the relativity of the civil service system, it is possible that in a unique situation (reprisal for protected activity such as previously filing a discrimination complaint or blowing the whistle) an employee might be able to force a supervisor to explain why a DP was initiated.

Therefore, even though proof is not required by law, it is a good idea for the supervisor to be able to "articulate" the reason for the DP, to give a bona fide reason for its implementation. And articulation does not mean boxes of documentation or even months of observation. At a minimum, a defensible articulation would be a two or three paragraph narrative drafted by the immediate supervisor at the time of DP implementation that gives the supervisor's reasons for DP initiation.

The narrative is best when it is specific, with dates and even witnesses, if relevant. For example, a good narrative would say things such as, "On March 16, Ed turned in his report on the Smith case, even though I had told him that the report was due March13. The report (copy attached) had several typos and had to be returned to him for rework." This is a better statement than one that says, "Ed often turns in reports late."

Once drafted, the pre-DP narrative should be retained by the supervisor (or employee relations). It should not be given to the employee. The only time it is relevant would be if the employee were to file a discrimination complaint alleging reprisal for EEO activity or a claim of whistleblower retaliation. It will not be required if the employee files some other sort of claim of discrimination because the Equal Employment Opportunity Commission (EEOC) has ruled that DP initiations are preliminary events and cannot be the subject of a routine discrimination complaint.

Element 3. Implement a Demonstration Period.

Once an employee has had a reasonable period of time to adjust to any new standard, as soon as that employee's performance becomes unacceptable in any one critical element, the supervisor should implement a Demonstration Period (DP). For the purposes of evaluating performance as it relates to retention, the supervisor should ignore any non-critical elements, as they are unrelated to the requirements for an unacceptable performance action. Deficient performance in any one critical element is all the catalyst necessary to initiate a DP.

Initiation of a DP requires the drafting of a formal DP Initiation Memo to the employee from the immediate supervisor. That memo should contain the following five sections:

1. **Notification to the employee that the supervisor has determined his performance to be unacceptable.** The supervisor should not do a lot of justifying or explaining as to his determination because the issuance of a DP cannot be challenged in any forum (with a limited exception of reprisal, discussed above, or an unusual collective bargaining agreement). Although this section can be a simple declarative conclusory statement of one or two sentences, some supervisors like to add a couple of examples of hypothetical poor performance to help the employee understand what he is doing wrong. Your particular situation will determine your approach. Just remember – the less you write, the less chance to make a mistake.

2. **Identification of the critical element(s) causing the problem.** The employee has a right to know in which of his many standards he is failing AND what level of performance he must attain to keep his job. The best approach is to reference the standard by number, then attach a copy of the employee's performance plan to the DP Initiation Memo. Make sure that the description of the minimal level of acceptable performance in the critical element is clear. This can be done by stating either the unacceptable level (e.g., three or more late reports in any five work-day period) or stating the minimally acceptable level (e.g., no more than two late reports in any five work-day period). So long as the line between acceptable and unacceptable performance is clearly delineated, the letter will be defensible.

3. **Warning that failure to attain acceptable performance will result in removal from the position.** This is not the time to muck around; this is the time to be very serious. Do not use equivocal language. By law, the supervisor must remove an employee who is performing unacceptably. That can be done by reassignment, demotion, or

termination. The employee should be apprised of this outcome so that there is no question as to what is going on. Perhaps one of the reasons that placement on a DP is relatively successful at retaining an acceptably-performing employee is because of this in-your-face notice that the employee's job is on the line. Statistically, about a third of employees who are placed on a DP each year are able to keep their jobs because they demonstrate acceptable performance.

4. **Offering of assistance.** An offer of on-going assistance from the supervisor during the DP can go a long way to convince a reviewing judge that you are not biased against the employee and that you sincerely wanted him to improve. In addition, if you set up a weekly meeting with the employee during the DP to discuss his performance, it becomes very hard for the employee to complain he did not know what was expected of him. We like to start DPs on Mondays, and have the first feedback meeting that Friday. It may not be the way you would prefer to spend your Friday afternoons, but a standing weekly meeting to discuss progress and problems is a very desirable addition to any performance action.

5. **Setting the length of the DP.** A DP lasts a finite period of time; from the date the letter is given to the employee to some date in the future that terminates the period during which the employee is being given an opportunity to demonstrate acceptable performance. This is the aspect of an unacceptable performance action which is most often used inefficiently! The law says that a DP should last a "reasonable" period of time. Unfortunately, too many agencies, either through a desire to be very careful or a misunderstanding of the law (or through union negotiations) have decreed that a DP should be at least 60 days in length, or 90 days, or some other arbitrary period of time not necessarily related to the specific critical element on which the employee is deficient. MSPB has approved a DP as short as 17 days, and has found only one DP to have been too short, and that was

for only three days. Setting a DP at 30 days is both reasonable and defensible.

The White House felt so strongly about this matter that the most recent Executive Order to address this issue requires that agencies generally set a DP at 30 days. "Generally" allows for exceeding 30 days should the employee be on approved sick leave during the period or for some other unforeseen occurrence. Given the mandates of the White House and the direction that the case law has taken, we strongly recommend that you establish the length of the DP no longer than 30 days.

Sometimes a supervisor will say, "Oh, a 30-day DP is too short. Dr. Dean does very important high-level work. His position descriptions essentially says, 'Cures cancer.' A 30-day DP will never work with him because his projects take many months to complete." The trick in this situation that will allow for you to use a 30-day DP is to avoid focusing on the long-term aspects of the work and ask yourself, "What do I want Dr. Dean to do in the next four weeks?" Every big project is made up of many smaller steps. Yes, we want him to cure cancer, but to get to that point, there must be preliminary planning, testing, and organization. Once you can answer the question as to what you want him to do in the next month, you have yourself a nice 30-day DP.

Caution: A few agencies have policies that require that the supervisor engage in significant "pre-DP" activity, sometimes even requiring what effectively is a "mini-DP" before the non-performing employee can be placed on a true DP. The recent EO prohibits agencies from having these sorts of policies. You agency should no longer require pre-DP mini-DPs.

Some agencies by collective bargaining agreement set DP minimums at three to four times the 30-day length recommended here. Some CBAs require mini-pre-DPs. If your agency is one of those, you must satisfy those unique requirements prior to implementing the DP described here, at least until your agency can negotiate with the union away from those provisions.

Element 4. Manage the DP.

Once the DP begins, you probably will want to devote some portion of each day to documenting the employee's performance (another good reason to keep the DP short). It is probably a good idea to keep a DP log or diary of some type in which you record the employee's accomplishments and job assignments, and your evaluation of the results. In addition, you will want to include any related matters that come up during this period. Was the employee absent on emergency or unapproved leave? Did the workflow change for some unexpected reason? Did customers or coworkers complain about the employee's performance? Keeping contemporaneous notes of what happens during the DP can be very good evidence if you need to defend your actions on appeal.

By the way, remember that your notes may one day wind up as documentary evidence in an administrative or court proceeding, proceedings often open to the public. It is a best practice to keep your DP notes separately from other notes and appointments you may be keeping in a diary or daily log. You probably do not want a copy of your Day Timer entered into evidence, especially if it contains annotations about doctor's appointments or other personal matters.

Also, remember that the DP is a period of time to demonstrate acceptable performance. It is not a time for employees to learn how to do their jobs. Some supervisors will send employees to training or allow practice time to develop skills (e.g., typing) during a DP. While that may be a good management approach attempting to help the employee get up to speed, it is not a requirement of law.

A DP can be terminated early if it becomes apparent that the employee will not be able to perform acceptably by the projected ending date. For example, if the performance standard states that three or more late reports during any 30-day period is unacceptable, and the employee has three late reports by week two of a 30-day DP, the supervisor can terminate the DP immediately propose the employee's removal based on unacceptable performance. There is no employee entitlement to the full period of the DP specified in the DP initiation letter (unless your collective bargaining agreement unfortunately says otherwise). That's why the best DP Initiation Memos sate that "The Demonstration Period will last *up to* 30 days."

During the DP, the supervisor should be extra careful to treat the employee with respect and to avoid giving anyone the impression that placement on the DP was motivated by ulterior motives (e.g., whistleblower reprisal, race discrimination, payback for aggressive union activity). We know that you would not be motivated by any improper reasons; however, it is not us that you have to convince. The last thing you want to have happen is to have to defend some off-the-cuff remark made during a DP that might even suggest that you are doing anything improper. You do not have to be the employee's best friend, but you really should be serious, concerned, and constructive.

Here's a trick from our personal practice of providing legal advice to agency managers. When we are working with a supervisor who has DP-ed an employee and who has set up weekly feedback meetings during the DP, that supervisor sends us an email or gives us a call after each meeting. We discuss what happened and the supervisor gives us the details of any instances of unacceptable performance that occurred that week. And right then, we begin to draft a proposed removal letter that incorporates those instances. We hope we never need it, because we hope the employee does not perform unacceptably. But drafting the tentative removal letter in weekly installments as the DP progresses accomplishes three important goals:

1. By updating the draft proposed removal letter and sending it to the supervisor for review each week, the supervisor begins to learn what will be need from a legal standpoint to propose removal should removal become necessary.
2. These weekly exchanges help your advisor better understand the nature of the work, thereby allowing the advisor to better compose the final letters, and to represent the agency at hearing.
3. As we approach the end of the fourth week, we have 75% of the draft removal proposal already completed. After getting the

supervisor's feedback from the final meeting, it won't take much time to finish the draft of the proposed removal and have it ready for the supervisor to issue on the 31st day.

Element 5. Make and implement a decision.

As the DP draws to a close, you are probably becoming aware as to whether the employee will reach the minimally acceptable level or will be rated as unacceptable. Do not wait until the DP is over to start contemplating you action. Several days before the end of the DP, meet with your advisers and start drafting a letter to issue at the termination of the DP if you have not done so already. Your goal should be to issue an end-of-DP letter (either proposing removal or notifying the employee of satisfactory completion of the DP) the day after the DP period is over. This is not a legal requirement, but simply good management given our goal of keeping this action as compact and as expedited as is reasonable and fair. There is no benefit to delaying your decision and its implementation much beyond the last day of the DP.

Your decision will be one of two options. As to the employee's performance as measured against the critical element(s) specified in the DP Initiation Memo, the employee will have performed either:

Acceptably, or
Unacceptably.

There is no in-between in this decision, no equivocation, only one of the two black-or-white alternatives. Whichever option you choose, you should draft and issue the employee a letter.

If performance was acceptable, you should give the employee a letter that says that he has performed satisfactorily during the DP, and that the DP period is now complete. If you are of the mood, you might even make that statement into a congratulatory note. It all depends on your style and the employee's performance during the DP. However, more importantly, you want to put the employee on notice of a very important twist in the unacceptable performance regulations:

If an employee's performance becomes unacceptable on the same critical element that was the subject of a DP within one year of the beginning of the DP, the supervisor can immediately initiate an action to remove the employee.

Before this principle was in place, some poorly performing employees took advantage of the old "DP roller coaster." Their performance would be unacceptable, they would be put on a DP, their performance would come up to acceptable, and then after the DP was over, their performance would once more slip to unacceptable, thereby requiring the initiation of another DP. Up and down they would go, hoping to reach retirement before they ran out of DPs. The current case law allows you to foreclose the roller coaster effect, and effectively place the employee on a one-year probationary period dating from the beginning of the DP. If the employee is successful during a DP, give him a congratulations memo, and also say something like, "Should your performance on this critical element again become unacceptable before April 14 of next year [assuming that the first day of the DP was April 15 this year], I will initiate immediate steps to remove you from your position for unacceptable performance."

Alternatively, if the employee's performance during the DP was unacceptable, you must take action to remove the employee from the position. There are two ways you can do this:

> **Reassignment** - You always retain the right to reassign an employee as long as your reason for doing so is for legitimate government reasons. If an employee is an unacceptable performer in one position, but is otherwise a decent employee, perhaps reassignment into another position which might be more compatible with the employee's (limited) skills would be in the best interest of the government. Frankly, though, if reassignment was a viable option for the employee, many supervisors would have chosen to do that prior to going to the trouble to implement a DP. However, if a position is available at the conclusion of the DP that might be an acceptable match between the employee's

abilities and the requirements of the job, reassignment to another position at the same grade and pay should be a first consideration.

Demotion or termination - If there is no appropriate reassignment position available, the supervisor, by law, must demote or remove the employee. Of course, as we will discuss in detail in Chapter Eight, the employee can voluntarily resign or accept another job and no formal action on the part of the supervisor is called for. Absent that relatively pleasant alternative, either a demotion or a termination is called for at this stage.

You probably remember our discussion in Chapter Two about the Douglas Factors and how one of the Five Fundamental Elements of every discipline action is a requirement that the supervisor defend his penalty selection. If the Board decides that the penalty in a misconduct removal is too severe, it will mitigate that penalty and order that it be replaced with a lesser penalty; for example, a suspension may be ordered in place of a removal.

That can never happen in an unacceptable performance removal. Congress specifically sheltered the supervisor's decision from challenge on appeal as to the appropriate action to take when confronted with an unacceptable performer. If the agency fires the unacceptable performer, the employee might argue on appeal that he should have been demoted rather than terminated based the following facts:

He has worked for the agency for 20 years with no discipline;
He has received an Outstanding rating for 18 of those 20 years in a previously-held lower-graded position;
The agency has 20 current vacancies in the lower-graded position he previously held; and
The agency has been recruiting unsuccessfully to fill those lower-graded positions for over a year.

Even though these appear to be very compelling facts suggesting the agency should have demoted the employee back into the position he previously held, the Board and the courts will never even consider this argument. The decision to fire rather than to demote is solely within the province of the agency [As is the law now for both misconduct and performance removals at the VA.].

Hardball Option: If you are in the mood to play a little hardball, there is an appealing way that you can take advantage of this aspect of the law. Assume that the employee has failed the DP and that you as the immediate supervisor are considering whether to demote or to remove. You have a position available at a lower level, but you are not sure the employee should not be fired instead. As the first line supervisor, you could propose a removal action based on the unacceptable performance during the DP and be perfectly within your rights. At the same time, you could let it be known to the deciding official that you would not have an objection to the employee being demoted instead to the lower level position you have available.

This approach leaves an interesting option for the deciding official. Assume that after the employee's response to the proposed removal, the deciding official is leaning toward a demotion rather than the proposed removal. He can then approach the employee (probably through his staff in some informal manner) and ask the employee if he would be willing to accept a demotion rather than a termination in exchange for waiving his rights to challenge the action through appeal or through a grievance. If the employee says "yes" (and most employees would, given the option of losing their jobs altogether), the agency has managed to avoid the expense and risk of an appeal that just might result in the employee being restored to work, with back pay and attorney fees. If the employee says "no," you are no worse off than if you had proposed a demotion from the beginning. The deciding official can still implement a demotion instead of a removal, or even go for the removal, if that is his decision. Without an appellate review of the penalty, the agency is free to do whatever it feels it needs to do in the best interest of the government.

Getting a little squeamish, are we? Concerned that this aggressive approach just doesn't seem "right" somehow? Well, let us assure you, once this case gets to court, you will not see the employee's junk-yard-dog lawyer sitting on his hands worrying about doing what is "right." He is going to be probing every weakness in your case, trying to win the appeal for his client. That is his ethical responsibility, and the best ones do it very well. By the time you get to this point when dealing with a problem employee, you should consider every avenue legally available to you to do what is in the best interest of the government. Yes, proposing a removal when you are willing to accept a demotion is hardball employee relations. But it is perfectly legal and appropriate employee relations so long as your motives are pure and you do not violate any due process rights of the employee.

OK, now you know that the employee has performed unacceptably during the DP and that you are not going to reassign him. Given that you are now left with initiating a formal action to terminate or demote the employee, you need to know the procedures for implementing that decision. That is what the next chapter is all about - how to terminate a bad government employee.

Chapter 4
The Removal Procedures

Whether you are firing someone for misconduct or for unacceptable performance, the procedures are roughly the same. Although the procedures discussed here are specific to the federal government, they should also parallel procedures found in most state and local governments, and even in private industry, especially in workplaces in which employees are represented by a union.

For ease of discussion, we will discuss the procedures for removing an employee from a federal government position. We will use variations of the terms "termination," "removal," and "firing" to indicate the same thing. However, you should be aware that although we discuss only removal actions, these same procedures in general apply if you are suspending an employee without pay or demoting the employee to a lower-graded position.

There are usually five steps involved in every removal action:

1. The investigation
2. The proposal letter
3. The response period

4. The decision letter
5. The appeal options

Step 1. Investigation

Many years ago, there was a regulatory provision that *required* a supervisor to conduct a thorough investigation prior to initiating a removal action for misconduct. Some actions were reversed simply for failure to conduct an adequate investigation even though the employee actually committed the charged offense. Today, the regulations do not require an investigation, but most supervisors will engage in fact finding of some sort prior to proposing a removal.

For unacceptable performance removals, there is no investigation. The DP period, discussed in the previous chapter, provides the supervisor with all of the information needed to take the action. However, when working with a disciplinary case, the supervisor usually needs to collect facts. In some situations, the only facts needed are the supervisor's personal observations. You saw the employee coming back to work from lunch two hours late. Make a contemporaneous note to remind yourself later exactly what you saw, and you have enough facts to take an action.

Other times the supervisor is not present when the misconduct occurs. When this happens, the supervisor may need to conduct a relatively formal investigation to get statements from witnesses to the misconduct if there are any available. Perhaps there was a fist fight in the workplace. Coworkers and others who may have been in the workplace at the time can be questioned about what happened. Sometimes the supervisor will ask the questions himself and other times the agency will appoint a trained investigator to conduct the interviews. In either event, the individual asking the questions usually takes notes as to what the witness says in response to the questions, and drafts a statement for the witness to review, edit, and sign under oath as to his version of the events. Occasionally, the investigator will run into one of three problems when questioning coworkers. Here's how to handle those challenges:

1. The employee who does not want to get involved – Sometimes coworkers will be hesitant to cooperate in an investigation because they fear that their involvement will anger the employees who are the subject of the investigation. Sometimes coworkers just do not like the supervisor who is conducting the investigation. It does not matter. Employees do not have the right to withhold information relative to a workplace incident and their cooperation is not necessarily voluntarily. A coworker who refuses to answer questions relative to a workplace incident may be subjected to discipline for insubordination, and can even be terminated. Usually, a gentle reminder of this fact is enough to get cooperation. If not, the employee's supervisor will have to decide how valuable the expected testimony would be and what discipline, if any, might be warranted.

2. The employee who asserts his "Fifth Amendment Privilege" – In our society, unlike most societies in the world, an individual cannot be forced to testify against himself in a criminal matter. That right is embodied in the Fifth Amendment to the U.S. Constitution and is probably one of the first rights we learned of as children watching TV programs. An employee who has engaged in workplace misconduct may well think that he does not have to give a statement because of this Constitutional protection against self-incrimination.

Well, that is an easy mistake to make. Unfortunately for the misbehaving employee, the Fifth Amendment protects against self-incrimination only in criminal matters. An administrative investigation is usually not a criminal matter, so an employee would have no right to refuse to answer questions based on the Fifth.

However, occasions might arise in which the questions being asked relative to workplace misconduct also would relate to possible criminal charges, either currently pending or that could conceivably be brought in the future. If that is the case, the employee is within his rights to refuse to answer questions. As a government supervisor, even though you are not (necessarily) a law enforcement official, when you ask questions of an individual, you are acting on behalf of the government. Therefore, the right to avoid self-incrimination kicks in, and an employee who sincerely believes his answer might incriminate him in a crime can justifiably refuse to answer.

There two ways to handle this:

1. *Explain the consequences of refusing to answer* – An employee who says he "takes the Fifth" should first be told that the Fifth Amendment protections apply only if there is a question of a crime being committed. Sometimes that will be enough to get the employee to participate. However, if he continues to assert the Fifth, you can say something like, "OK, I realize that you are choosing not to answer because you believe that to do so might incriminate you in a criminal matter. However, be aware that I will be collecting a lot of statements and other facts relative to this incident and that this may be your only chance to get your side of the story into the record. You can continue to refuse to cooperate and I will have to make my decision based on the other evidence I collect, or you can choose to participate by answering my questions and telling me your version of what happened. In addition, you should know that your decision not to answer my questions will be considered when deciding whether discipline for you is warranted." The lawyers call this a Garrity Warning, and many times such a warning will get the employee to see the light and to participate in the interview.

2. *Give the employee a Kalkines Warning* – An employee has a Fifth Amendment right to remain silent and thereby to avoid self-incrimination only when he has a reasonable belief that he might be subject to criminal charges based on his answer. Many types of relatively minor workplace misbehavior may well be considered crimes and can thereby give the employee a valid reason for staying quiet. However, that "reasonable belief" can be disabled if the employee is assured that the government will not prosecute him criminally based on truthful answers he gives

in a misconduct investigation. To give an employee such an assurance, the government authority responsible for prosecuting the criminal activity can waive its right to prosecute, thereby removing the employee's reasonable belief once he is informed of that waiver. If an agency is confronted with an employee who asserts the Fifth Amendment and refuses to answer questions during an investigation, it should consider discussing the matter of developing a Kalkines Warning with the responsible district attorney or federal prosecutor to force the employee to participate.

3. The employee who wants a union representative present prior to answering any questions – Employees in collective bargaining units (i.e., unionized employees) have the right by law to have union representatives in meetings convened by management in two situations. First, a union representative has a right to be present when management convenes a meeting in which working conditions are discussed. Second, an employee has a right to have a union representative present in an investigation in which the employee is the target of potential discipline. This latter type of meeting is known as a Weingarten meeting, and the right to be represented in a Weingarten meeting must be told to employees at least annually.

The first situation should not arise in an investigatory meeting. When suspected misconduct is being investigated, it is very unlikely that there will be any sort of discussion of working conditions. Therefore, the union will not need to be notified and allowed to participate.

The second situation will arise much more frequently, especially when the employee being interviewed is the one who is suspected of committing the misconduct. When a targeted employee exercises his Weingarten right and asks for a union representative, you should not continue the questioning until a representative has been obtained or the employee decides to waive the right. The following might help you through this situation should it occur:

- Although the employee has a right to a union representative, you are not obligated to continue the interview with a union representative present. Much as we suggested in the discussion of the Kalkines Warning, above, you may simply want to tell the employee that you will continue with the interview only if he waives his right to have a representative present, that this might be his only chance to get his side of the story into the record.

- The employee has a right to a union representative, but not necessarily to a representative of his choosing. He may want the union president there even though the president works at a facility many miles away and is currently on leave for three weeks. You are perfectly within your rights to deny the request to have the president attend and to ask that the union and employee identify a representative who is more convenient.

- You need not adjourn the interview and reconvene later when the representative is available. The employee can be kept in the interview room while a representative is brought in.

- Although the representative has the right to be present, he does not have the right to obstruct the interview, to ask questions, or to record the interview, and he can be ejected if he does.

Even though you now know the legal principles that guide these interviews, you should work closely with the agency's labor relations staff when deciding how to handle these situations. As mentioned previously, labor relations is as much art as it is law, and your agency may have ways of dealing with these situations that fit best into its overall plan for labor harmony. Check with the pros.

By the way, employees who are not in bargaining units have no right of representation during investigatory meetings. The employee who refuses to participate in an interview without his lawyer being present just may find himself consulting his lawyer relative to an appeal of a removal based on insubordination. Agencies are free, of course, to allow a non-union employee to have a representative during an interview, but there is no requirement they do so.

Written statements taken during an investigation are best if they are signed, dated, and attested to under oath or affirmation and the penalty of perjury. However, some agencies hesitate to do this because there is a question as to exactly who has the authority to administer an oath. In the federal sector, this problem can be avoided by adding a statement that the person giving the statement asserts it is truthful and is aware that it is a crime to lie during an official government investigation:

> *I attest that the above statement is accurate and truthful to the best of my knowledge and that I might be subjected to the criminal sanctions found at 18 U.S.C. 1001 for not telling the truth in this matter, and to the penalty for perjury.*

Placing this statement immediately above the interviewee's signature gives significant weight to the written statement and is just as good from an evidentiary standpoint as is a sworn notarized affidavit, while being much less trouble to obtain.

In particularly delicate situations, the supervisor should consider video recording statements given by witnesses to acts of misconduct. Perfectly adequate video cameras can be bought for less than $200 these days, or found on your smart phone. A video recorded statement of an individual who is no longer available to testify can be a very powerful piece of evidence. In addition, videotaping can occur in the workplace where the incident took place and can include visual references to equipment, spaces, and distances. Just be sure that the witness asserts that he knows he must tell the truth and can be charged criminally if he does not (or just have him take an oath of truthfulness and worry later about who really has the authority to administer the oath).

Step 2. Proposal Letter

Once the investigation is completed (or the DP has expired) the immediate supervisor in most agencies will be responsible for issuing a proposed removal letter. Because this document is fundamental to the final action and will receive close scrutiny on appeal, it is usually drafted by an agency employee relations expert to make sure that it is technically accurate. However, the factual statements in the letter are statements that the supervisor who issues the letter will have to swear to as accurate under oath at hearing, so it is imperative that the supervisor agree with its contents.

The letter will have five sections:

Heading – The from-to initial section of the memo/letter should include not only the names of the supervisor and the employee, but also their official titles as found in their position descriptions or the agency's official organizational chart. Usually, you will include the grade of the employee because the action may well be relevant to the pay grade.

Purpose Statement – Right up front, say what the letter is all about, "By this letter, I am proposing that you be removed from your position for the following reason:" or something like that. Do not wait until the end to spring it on the employee.

Reason Statement – In a misconduct removal, this will be where you delineate the charges and specifications on which the removal is based. For example, "AWOL: From March 12 through March 20, you were absent from work without approved leave (AWOL) a total of 56 hours. You did not request leave prior to this absence and you have failed to explain your absence since your return to work last Tuesday."

In an unacceptable performance action, the Reason Statement will be a recitation of the critical element that was the subject of the DP followed by a description of the incidents that demonstrated the unacceptable performance. For example:

> *Critical Element Four, Minimally Successful Level: No more than three late reports in any 30-day period.*
>
> *You are required to file three weekly reports with me by the close of business every Friday. Those reports are known as the X, Y, and Z Reports. Your 30-day DP commenced on March 1. On March 7 you submitted the X report to me two days after the preceding Friday,*

> *thereby making it a late report. On March 15, you filed the Y report to me three days late, and on March 27, you filed both the Y and Z report to me one day beyond the weekly Friday deadline. During this 30-day period, you filed four reports late. Therefore, your performance as measured by this critical element is unacceptable.*

Reason Statements may be longer than these and more detailed. However, statements this concise will suffice to put the employee on notice of the supervisor's reason for proposing the action, and thereby satisfy the due process requirement of notice. Without proper notice, the courts have held that a tenured government employee cannot properly defend himself and cannot be terminated.

Technically, the Reason Statement for a misconduct removal (but not a performance removal) should address the factors the proposing official is relying upon to select a particular penalty. The best practice is to complete a Douglas Factor Worksheet (sample found in the Appendix), attached it to the Proposal Letter, and reference the worksheet attachment in this section of the letter; e.g., "In selecting the penalty for your misconduct, I relied on the penalty factors as described in the attached worksheet."

Response Statement – The proposal letter will notify the employee of the opportunity to respond to the proposal by addressing arguments and documentary evidence to the agency official empowered to decide whether to enact the proposal. Usually, this "deciding official" is the employee's second-level supervisor, but the agency is relatively free to designate just about any management official it chooses as the deciding official. In this section, the employee should be told who the deciding official is, how long he has to make a response, what form the response can take (e.g., oral, written, or both), and how to make an appointment to make an oral response.

> *Practice Hint:* A better practice is to set a date and time for the oral response with the deciding official right in the proposal letter. That way, the agency avoids potential problems if the employee claims to have had trouble otherwise scheduling a response with the deciding official.

Rights Statement - In this section, sometimes incorporated into the Response Statement section above, the employee will be told he has a right to a representative and how to review any evidence on which the proposal is based. The better practice is for the supervisor to attach to the proposal letter all the materials relied upon in making the decision to propose removal. Again, doing so proactively avoids any claims that the employee was somehow denied the documents relied upon.

In addition to these five sections, the proposal letter in a removal action should notify the employee that he is being placed into a paid leave status and that he is not to return to the workplace until he receives further instruction. For many years, this was an awkward step in some agencies. OPM has had antiquated regulations in place for a long time that say that the employee should be retained in his regular position during the notice period of a proposed removal.

Well, that is just stupid. Anyone with any common sense can see the danger in allowing an employee to have continued access to a federal worksite after he has been told he is about to be fired. The Bureau of Labor Statistics estimates that every work day of the year, two people in our country are killed by a coworker. We can never predict what someone will do who has been stressed by being given a proposed removal letter. In addition, we are not likely to get much work out of someone who has a proposed removal hanging over his head. And, it makes no sense to allow an about-to-be fired employee to have 30 days of access to a government workspace, with all that secret information on the computers and easily-stolen property sitting around just waiting to be sold on Craig's List.

In December 2016, Congress recognized this problem. Although the old standby of placing the employee on Administrative Leave is no longer available, we now have a law that allows an agency to place an employee who has been given a proposed removal on something called Notice Leave. Depending on your agency, you may have to complete some paperwork to do this. However, as long as you can honestly conclude that retaining the employee in a work status "jeopardizes a government interest," then you can invoke Notice Leave for the duration of the period it takes the

Deciding Official to issue a decision. This is a life-or-death issue. For your own protection, get the employee out of the workplace once you have proposed removal.

Step 3. Response Period

Proposed removal letters establish two time frames:

1. A period during which the employee can make his response to the proposed removal (at least seven days after the proposal is issued), and

2. A period during which the supervisor will consider the proposed action prior to issuing a decision (in a misconduct case the deciding official can make a decision any time after the employee responds, but any removal decision cannot be implemented sooner than 30 days after the proposal is issued; in a performance case the deciding official may not make a decision until after the conclusion of the 30-day notice period).

Although seven days is the minimum period of time that an employee can be given to respond to a proposed termination, an agency can extend this period, either ad hoc or by collective bargaining agreement.

If an oral response is given, the deciding official may choose to hear it himself or designate another management official to hear it in his place. There is no right for employees to have witnesses testify at an oral response, and most agencies do not allow witness testimony, although the submission of written sworn statements in support of the employee is common. Employees may be represented by an attorney, a union official, or just about anyone else at the oral response meeting, so long as there is no conflict of position in the representation. For example, an employee whose removal has been proposed cannot be represented by a government management official.

The management official who is hearing the response or someone present in the meeting on his behalf should keep notes of the employee's oral response. It is not necessary to give the employee an opportunity to review and make comments on the notes taken, although some agencies do. The notes taken during the response, the employee's written response and accompanying evidence, and the evidence and rationale submitted in support of the proposed removal by the immediate supervisor provide the information necessary to implement the proposed removal.

Step 4. Decision Letter

Although this is the document that actually terminates the employee, it is the easiest to draft. Essentially, for a misconduct action it needs to say no more than, "After careful consideration of the charges specified in the proposal letter dated April 1 and your oral and written responses, I have concluded that the charges are sustained. Based on my consideration of the relevant penalty factors, I have decided to implement the proposed removal." For an unacceptable performance removal, you might say something like, "After careful consideration of your performance during the DP, I have concluded that your performance as measured against Critical Element Two of your performance standards was unacceptable. Therefore, I have decided to implement the proposed removal." Inform the employee that the effective date of the removal is the end of the day, include a notification of the employee's rights to appeal the removal, and you're done.

Keep this awkward statutory distinction in mind:

- In an *adverse action removal* (e.g., misconduct), the Deciding Official can issue a decision anytime after the employee responds. For example, if the employee responds on day seven, the Decision Letter can be issued day eight. However, the removal cannot be implemented, and the employee has to be kept in a pay status, until 30 days have passed since the Proposal Letter was issued.

- In an *unacceptable performance removal*, the Deciding Official cannot issue the Decision Letter until 30 days have passed since

> removal was proposed. The effective date of the termination, and the employee's removal from the payroll, should be the date the Decision Letter is issued.

What, you say!?! No prior warning, no 7 or 15 or 30 days to say goodbye to coworkers and to get adjusted to unemployment? Do we really mean to say that the employee can, nay, should be terminated immediately? Yes, Virginia, that is exactly what we are saying. The employee is not entitled by law or regulation to any specific period of warning between the decision and the date it is actually implemented, so there is no requirement that a warning be given.

The White House has found a need to address the timing of the decision letter in an Executive Order. Unfortunately, some agencies over the years have been waiting months and months after a proposal to issue a final decision to terminate. A few cases have gone on for more than a year, with the employee in a pay status the whole time. As of today, the President's EO requires deciding officials to issue a decision on a proposed removal:

- No later than 19 days after the employee responds, and
- No more than 30 days after the date of the proposal notice.

Agencies are required to report the names of deciding officials who exceed these time frames to the White House. You won't lose the case if you are late, but you won't make any friends in the administration, either.

> *A note on Executive Orders. Throughout this text we have made references to EOs that currently affect the accountability procedures in the Executive Branch. Keep in mind that EOs sometimes come and go, depending on who is sitting in the Oval Office. Trust your advisors for advice on what the current status of any EO is prior to taking action with a problem employee.*

Step 5. Appeal Options

In the federal government, a terminated employee has several options when deciding whether and with whom to file an appeal to challenge the termination. In other government organizations, there often is an appeal to a state board or commission that parallels the rights afforded to federal employees. The appeal avenues open to most terminated federal employees are (in order of popularity):

U.S. Merit Systems Protection Board – The Board traces its heritage to the establishment of the original U.S. Civil Service Commission in 1883. Its primary mandate since that time has been to oversee the fairness of the merit system mainly by hearing the appeals of terminated or otherwise seriously disciplined federal employees, and thereby creating an extensive body of case law that controls the federal workplace.

A terminated federal employee, referred to as an appellant, has the right to a hearing before an administrative judge at MSPB to challenge his dismissal. In that hearing, witnesses are called and subjected to both direct and cross examination, evidence is entered into the record, and the representatives of the agency and the appellant make arguments to the judge. The process is almost identical to a trial in a criminal court except at a slightly less formal level, lower burdens of proof, and no juries. The agency will have to go forward first and submit adequate evidence to prove that the removal action was justified (see the Fundamental Elements discussions in Chapter 2). The appellant will have the opportunity to cross-examine the agency's witnesses and to present witnesses and evidence on his own behalf.

There are six stages in the initial MSPB process:

1. The terminated employee must file a *written appeal* with the Board. The agency's termination decision letter contains information for the employee as to how to file an appeal electronically online at www.mspb.gov. We now refer to the former employee as the "appellant."

2. One of the administrative judges who works in the regional office geographically responsible for the site of the employee's former workplace will review the initial appeal and will issue an *acknowledgment order* that directs the appellant and the agency to do certain things. Primarily, it directs the agency to submit a file containing all of its evidence and argument regarding the employee's termination, and simultaneously initiates the "discovery" phase of the appeal proceedings. In addition, the agency and the appellant will be ordered to engage in settlement discussions. MSPB would rather that appeals settle than go to a hearing. Over 50% of Board appeals settle without a hearing.

3. *Discovery* is a period of time prior to hearing during which the agency and the appellant can get information about the case from each other by requiring certain questions be answered in writing, certain documents be produced, and by requiring certain individuals to answer questions in person and orally in a "deposition" setting. As a management official involved in the case, you may be required by the agency representative (either an attorney or a labor/employee relations specialist) to participate in these processes. Of the three, the deposition process is the most challenging for you because of the need to be honest, to answer questions posed by the appellant's representative in a forthright manner while not saying anything that will hurt the agency's case. Most every agency representative will prepare you extensively should you be called on to give a deposition.

4. About a week to ten days before the date of the hearing, the judge assigned to the case will require the representatives of both sides of the appeal to participate in a *pre-hearing telephone conference* to discuss the facts and law at issue, and to make certain preliminary rulings relative mainly to witnesses and evidence. By the time that conference is over, the agency representative (and the appellant's representative) will know in a much more focused way exactly what the judge believes

the case to be all about, and will have a relatively good idea as to the chances of success. If you are the proposing or deciding official, you should expect a briefing from the agency representative at this stage as to what he sees as the probable outcome of the appeal.

5. Around 60 to 75 days after the employee files the initial appeal, the judge will conduct a *hearing*. The hearing is usually held either in the Board's hearing room at the regional office if the regional office is located near the employee's last workplace, or it may be held in a courthouse if the location is other than one of the cities nationwide in which the Board has an office. Sometimes if no other facility is available, the agency will be asked to provide a hearing room. At other times, the hearing will be by video-conference. The hearing will proceed much as does a civil trial with witnesses being called, objections being made, and arguments between the representatives. The agency representative will meet with you and go over the questions he intends to ask you at hearing as well as the questions you can expect from the employee's representative.

    - If you are going to be called as a witness in a Board hearing, you may want to take a couple of hours to sit in as an observer at a Board hearing unrelated to your case. MSPB's hearings are public and your employee relations representative can arrange for you to attend one in preparation for your own testimony. Or, simply call the Board and ask for hearing dates and locations yourself: 202-653-MSPB.

6. After the hearing has concluded, the judge will issue a *decision* (referred to as an "Initial Decision" because it can be appealed). Sometimes the evidence and law are so clear that the judge will issue an oral "bench decision" right there in the hearing room after the witnesses have testified. More likely, however, you will receive a written decision within 30 days of the close of the hearing. MSPB has set a standard for completing its initial adjudication within 120 days of the filing of the

initial appeal, and it meets this standard better than 95% of the time. As for a success rate, only about one out of four or five agency actions is reversed at this level.

After the judge issues the initial decision, either side can appeal that decision to the three politically-appointed Board members in Washington, D.C. The Board members uphold the outcome ordered by the judge more than 90% of the time, so the chances are great that whatever the judge ruled will be the final outcome of the appeal. Final Board decisions (called an Opinion and Order or an O&O) can take up to a year or more in a complicated case. Less complex cases sometimes are decided in just a few weeks.

From the Board, the agency (with OPM's approval) or the employee can appeal the decision to the Federal Circuit Court of Appeals and even to the U.S. Supreme Court. Only about a dozen cases originating at MSPB have been heard by the Supreme Court in the past 40 years, and the Federal Circuit upholds the Board about 95% of the time. So, the bottom line is that whatever the judge decides is very likely to be the final outcome of the case, even though there could be adjudication which may drag on for years. Fortunately, your active involvement as the supervisor is required only through the hearing process. Even if the case goes all the way to the Supreme Court and takes four or five years to finally come to a conclusion, your direct involvement will most likely be over when the judge says to you, "The witness is excused."

U.S. Equal Employment Opportunity Commission – Notorious because of its complexity and inherent delays, the federal discrimination complaint process is a textbook example of good intentions resulting in bad results. Rather than taking about 100 to 120 days to get a decision from a judge as in an MSPB appeal, it may well take three or four years to get a similar judge's decision through the federal discrimination process. Part of this delay is a result of the several layers of procedures imposed and part is the result of historic under-funding for this process. Some might argue that if the procedure were more efficient, we simply would have more complaints filed.

Fortunately, that debate is not one we need to resolve. As a government supervisor, you simply need to know the procedures to expect should the employee you terminated challenge that action by filing a discrimination complaint with EEOC alleging that you have discriminated against him based on one of the civil rights categories (i.e., race, sex, age, disability, color, religion, genetics, national origin, or in reprisal for earlier EEO activity). In highly abbreviated form, those procedures are:

1. The terminated employee must first seek counseling from an agency-designated EEO Counselor.

2. The counselor conducts an informal investigation and provides the results to the employee.

3. If dissatisfied with the result of the counseling, the employee then files a formal complaint of discrimination with the agency.

4. The agency assigns or hires a trained investigator to formally investigate the complaint and to compile an extensive Report of Investigation.

5. The employee requests a written final agency decision, or requests a hearing with EEOC, where the matter is referred to an administrative judge in the responsible regional office.

6. The EEOC judge has to make a decision as to whether he will conduct a hearing or whether the hearing should be conducted by an MSPB judge (because the MSPB judges routinely deal with termination and other serious adverse action issues).

7. If the case is not sent to MSPB, the judge's decision can be appealed, by the employee or the agency, to a division of the EEOC called the Office of Federal Operations (OFO).

8. If either side does not like the OFO decision, it can ask OFO for reconsideration. Now the employee can jump down to step 14.

9. Picking up from step 6, if the case is remanded to MSPB, the six steps enumerated previously that describe the MSPB appeal process will take place.

8. Eventually, the three members of MSPB will issue a final decision.

10. The employee can then appeal the Board's final decision to EEOC in a process called a "mixed case" review (some would say a "mixed up" case review).

11. The Commission issues a decision either agreeing or disagreeing with the Board, and sends the case back to MSPB for reconsideration if it disagrees with the Board's decision.

12. If MSPB, after reconsideration, disagrees with EEOC, the matter is referred to the Special Panel, a governmental entity created solely to resolve these disputes.

13. The Special Panel issues a decision.

14. The employee can then take the case to federal district court where he is entitled to a trial "de novo" meaning that the court is not bound by any of the findings in the extensive administrative review process that got the case to this point, and the employee can present his case to a jury if he so chooses.

15. The district court's decision can be appealed to the appropriate federal circuit court and to the U.S. Supreme Court.

And you thought brain surgery and rocket science were challenging.

Arbitration – Arbitration is a process by which the parties to a disagreement (here that means the agency that fired the employee and the employee) agree to resolve the dispute by submitting the issue to an impartial third-party adjudicator. In government, this right to go to arbitration comes about only when a union represents the terminated employee and the union decides that arbitration is warranted; i.e., the employee cannot invoke arbitration unless the union consents.

The arbitration process is initiated by the employee filing a grievance with the agency. Each grievance process is unique because each is developed through the collective bargaining process. In general, however, a written grievance is required. After a review of the grievance by an agency official, if the agency decides not to grant the grievance, the union can invoke arbitration.

Once the union invokes arbitration, the agency representative and the union representative meet to select an arbitrator to hear the grievance. An arbitrator is essentially a contractor from the private sector hired to act as a judge in the case. Once an arbitrator is selected, he is notified of his selection and a date for the hearing is set. Unlike the procedures at MSPB and EEOC, there is not necessarily any great sharing of information between the parties prior to the hearing. As at MSPB, on the day of hearing the agency will go first because it has the burden of proving the fundamental elements of its case, witnesses will testify, evidence will be offered and entered into the record, and the representatives of each side will make competing arguments to the arbitrator.

Once the hearing concludes, the arbitrator will take several weeks or longer to draft a decision (called an "award") and will send it to the parties along with his bill. Usually, the union and the agency split the cost of the arbitration, although in some collective bargaining agreements, the loser of the arbitration pays all of the costs. The cost of a removal arbitration can easily exceed $20,000. As you can imagine, unions have to be selective in which cases they take to arbitration because of the cost.

Ideally, the decision of an arbitrator would be final and binding. A main purpose of an arbitration is to reduce the legal proceedings to a minimum so that the parties can reach closure quickly and get on with other things. However, in the federal sector, an arbitration award can be appealed by either side to the Federal Labor Relations Authority if it is alleged that the arbitrator's award violates federal law or does not otherwise draw its "essence" from the four corners of the union contract. If the employee claims discrimination based on any of the "civil rights" categories, he can appeal the arbitrator's decision to the Board members at MSPB. However, the Board shows deference to an arbitrator's judgment and will not substitute its conclusions for those of the arbitrator absent a clear error in interpreting civil service law or regulation.

U.S. Office of Special Counsel – Unlike the other independent agencies mentioned here, OSC is not a neutral adjudicator. Rather, it is more akin to a district attorney or independent prosecutor. It receives complaints, conducts investigations when appropriate, and files charges with MSPB when it believes that an agency has committed a prohibited personnel practice.

As a practical matter, as it relates to a terminated employee, OSC gets involved only when an employee files a written complaint, either by regular mail or electronically at www.osc.gov, and alleges that he is the victim of whistleblower reprisal. If OSC concludes that the complaint may be valid, it conducts an on-site investigation and reaches a conclusion as to whether whistleblower reprisal actually occurred. If it concludes that it did, it will approach the agency representative and try to convince the agency to cancel the removal. If the agency refuses, OSC will file two types of petitions with MSPB:

1. OSC will file a *corrective action* petition and ask that the Board agree with its conclusion that whistleblower reprisal occurred and direct the agency to reemploy the employee/complainant, and

2. OSC will file a *disciplinary action* petition and ask that the Board impose discipline against the management officials who engaged in the whistleblower reprisal. That discipline can include a reprimand, suspension, demotion, termination, debarment from future federal service, and a monetary fine of over a thousand dollars.

Should OSC decide to bring charges against you as the supervisor, your agency will not be allowed to defend you and you will either have to defend yourself or hire an attorney to represent you in the MSPB proceedings.

Do not worry too much, though. OSC rarely engages in this sort of prosecution.

Should OSC file a corrective action petition, the agency will have to defend its termination very much as it would if the employee had appealed directly to MSPB as described above.

Settlement – Strictly speaking, settlement is not an appeal option. However, every procedure discussed above, except arbitration, relies heavily on settlement to resolve complaints. In settlement, the agency and the employee agree to stop the appellate process and resolve the matter by entering into a contract in which each side gets something, and each side gives something. You should expect the judge assigned in your case at either EEOC or MSPB to put a fair amount of pressure on both sides to settle the appeal/complaint. When that happens, do not conclude that your case is necessarily weak. In court or in an administrative proceeding, the powers that be have concluded that settlement is better than adjudication, so you are going to see pressure to settle regardless of the merits of the removal.

Sometimes the parties to an appeal will agree to use a "mediator" to help reach a settlement. Do not confuse a mediator with an arbitrator. Whereas an arbitrator sits as a judge and decides who is right and who is wrong, a mediator has no such right-or-wrong concern. Rather, a mediator is there to help the employee and the agency think thorough options other than continuing with the adjudication, and to help the parties draw up a binding agreement that will resolve the matter to everyone's satisfaction.

The most common settlement of a termination is for the agency to agree to remove the termination from the employee's record in exchange for the employee to resign voluntarily. Sometimes a little money will pass from the agency to the employee to cover his attorney fees (maybe $5000 or so). Other agreements might allow the employee to be restored to employment (perhaps into a lower-graded position), but without back pay and with the understanding that he can be summarily terminated based on the slightest future act of misconduct or poor performance. Of course, settlements can take many forms and contain many provisions, a topic far beyond the scope of this text.

Once more, though, we have to look to the most recent Executive Order issued by the White House. For reasons not completely clear, the EO prohibits agencies from entering into settlement agreements that provide the employee a "clean record" i.e., removal of the termination documentation from the employee's official personnel file. As this text goes to press, agency representatives are wrestling with how to deal with this new Presidential restriction.

As a supervisor, you should be aware that a removal action you take may well settle without going through a full adjudication. You should not take this as an indication that there was anything wrong with what you did! Agencies decide to settle cases for many reasons that are unrelated to the merits of the underlying termination action. As mentioned above, about 20% of the appeals to MSPB result in the agency's action being set aside or modified. When the goal is to keep a fired employee off the rolls, and the agency can obtain that goal with 100% certainty by settling a case, it will probably do so rather than risk the 80% chance of success were the case to go through the entire appellate process. Think creatively as to what you would like to see as an acceptable result if you are involved in a settlement discussion, and be prepared to enter into a contract that guarantees your ultimate objective will be attained, although perhaps through an alternative process. Settlement is good. Use it to your advantage.

Now that you know the removal process and the optional appeal procedures, we will focus in the next chapter on one of the most challenging parts of a termination for misconduct - the combining of an acceptable charge with an appropriate penalty.

CHAPTER 5
PENALTY DEFENSE

Sometimes it seems as if proving the employee engaged in misconduct is the easiest part of a case. An agency can be successful when proving this fundamental aspect of a removal case, but have the removal mitigated by the Board to a suspension because it fails to establish that the charges were serious enough to warrant removal.

Although MSPB is a relatively stable institution, over the years observers have noticed a series of mood swings relative to penalty selection deference and mitigation. Some years the Board's judges will be relatively active when it comes to mitigating a removal by an agency, either by finding that the deciding official did not consider all the relevant Douglas Factors or simply by disagreeing with the deciding official's consideration of and weight given to the factors. In those years, it becomes a common occurrence to see a judge's decision that says something like, "Although I have found all the charges sustained, I conclude that the penalty of removal is unreasonable and mitigate the removal to a 30-day suspension."

In other years, the sitting Board members will embark on a course of sustaining the agency's selection of penalty in just about every case in which a judge below has mitigated the removal. Whether a particular trend will continue or change depends on who the next round of political appointees is at the Board (a member usually is replaced every two or three years). To understand where the Board stands on penalty mitigation at any given time, you must look to a series of recent decisions to determine the direction of any current trend.

Unfortunately, as this text goes to print, we have zero recent decisions on which we can rely to try to identify a penalty trend. As discussed previously in the Prologue, the White House and the Senate have allowed the Board to go forward with only one Board member for over two years. As one member cannot issue decisions, and because eventually three brand spanking new members will take office, currently we have no idea what direction MSPB's philosophy on mitigation will take in the future. The best we can do is to study trends from earlier times, and thereby appreciate the potential direction penalty mitigation might take whenever we again get an operating Board quorum.

The following is a selection of 20 or so decisions issued by MSPB in a particular time period in which penalty selection became a significant issue. Although a bit tedious to study, it is worth your while to review these holdings to see how this Board, and perhaps other Boards in the future, view the art of pairing a reasonable penalty with a good charge. In addition, if you are new to the business of disciplining, it will be helpful for you to see the sorts of misconduct for which government employees are terminated.

The following list of case holdings refers to actual decisions issued by MSPB and can be found on the web at www.mspb.gov by selecting the correct year from the "Search MSPB Decisions" screen and entering the name of the appellant into the search engine. Alternatively, if your agency has legal reference material available, refer to the series of West-published Board decisions known as the *Federal Merit Systems Reporter*. For example, *Campbell v. USPS*, 94 MSPR 646 can be found in volume 94 beginning on page 646 of the MSPR series. Or, if you are fortunate, your agency may have access to a commercial on-line database of Board decisions.

Although older, these cases are still typical of how the Board views penalty defense today.

Brown v. Army, AT-0752-03-0905-I-1 (May 28, 2004)

Charge: Unauthorized use of his government-issued travel card when he made 67 unauthorized charges.

Agency's Penalty: Removal

Judge's Penalty: Mitigated the removal to a 60-day suspension even though the appellant had a prior 60-day suspension for unauthorized use of a government vehicle.

Board's Penalty: Reinstated the removal. Among other things, the Board noted that when the appellant was asked at hearing whether it was a violation of regulation to use the travel card for personal expenses, he replied "It's a violation if they catch you." The Board found the response and a review of his testimony in general supported a finding that the appellant did not exhibit rehabilitative potential.

Campbell v. USPS, 94 MSPR 646 (2003)

Charge: Being in a non-pay status for more than a year.

Agency's Penalty: Removal

Judge's Penalty: Reversed the removal because the absences were approved and related to poor communication rather than a lack of work within the appellant's medical limitations.

Board's Penalty: Reinstated the removal. The Board stated, "Prolonged absences with no foreseeable end can provide a just cause for removal because it constitutes a burden that no employer can efficiently endure."

Carlton v. Justice, 95 MSPR 633 (2004)

Charge: Criminal conduct, conduct unbecoming a law enforcement officer, and lack of candor. All three charges stemmed from an event in which the appellant threw a vase at his wife, threw her down on the floor, choked her, pointed a gun at her, and then pointed a gun at himself.

Agency's Penalty: Removal

Judge's Penalty: Mitigation to a demotion. The judge did not sustain the criminal conduct charge and one specification of the lack of candor charge.

Board's Penalty: Reinstated the removal. The Board noted the deciding official's testimony that he considered other options short of removal, but decided that retaining appellant in a law enforcement position was not feasible given the egregious nature of the incident involving the wife, the appellant's guilty plea to a misdemeanor charge, the conditions of his probation, the continual denial of the misconduct by the appellant, and the effect of his guilty plea on his ability to testify credibly in court. The appellant's lack of candor reasonably caused the agency to have concerns about its ability to trust and have confidence in him. The misconduct was serious and raised valid concerns about the appellant's lack of judgment and impulse control and his abilities to perform the duties of his position.

Doe v. USPS, 95 MSPR 493 (2004)

Charge: Failure to follow instructions and delay of the mail.

Agency's Penalty: Removal

Judge's Penalty: Mitigation to a 45-day suspension.

Board's Penalty: Reinstated the removal. The Board rejected the appellant's argument that he was similarly situated to another employee who also had failed to follow the same supervisor's instructions and who received only a suspension. In order to be similarly situated, the appellant's employment situation must be nearly identical to that of the comparison employee in all relevant aspects. Here, although the appellant and the comparison employee shared the same job description and the same supervisor, they supervised different crafts.

Dogar v. DoD, 95 MSPR 52 (2003)

Charge: Falsifying documents and submitting a fraudulent travel claim.

Agency's Penalty: Removal

Judge's Penalty: Reversed the removal. The judge found that although much of the information the appellant submitted was inaccurate or unverifiable, the charges were not proven because the appellant genuinely believed he was entitled to be reimbursed for the amount claimed, and thus he did not defraud the agency.

Board's Penalty: Reinstated the removal. Even though only one of the four specifications of misconduct was sustained (falsification) and there were "a few mitigating factors" present, removal was warranted. Falsification is a serious offense, reflecting adversely on the employee's reliability, veracity, trustworthiness and ethical conduct. In addition, the record showed significant prevarication on the appellant's part during the investigation.

Dunn v. Air Force, 96 MSPR 166 (2004)

Charge: Engaging in conduct unbecoming a federal employee and exhibiting a lack of candor. The appellant left a Minuteman III Intercontinental Ballistic Missile sitting on an unlocked truck with the motor running in a public parking lot for 45 minutes.

Agency's Penalty: Removal

Judge's Penalty: Mitigated to a demotion. The judge faulted the deciding official for considering primarily the first Douglas Factor when selecting an appropriate penalty, the seriousness of the misconduct.

Board's Penalty: Reinstated the removal. The Board also considered primarily the seriousness of the misconduct and held that to do so was appropriate: "It can scarcely be argued that leaving a Minuteman III Intercontinental Ballistic Missile unattended in a public parking lot for any length of time is not a most serious offense." In spite of the employee's 28-year unblemished record, removal was warranted.

Faucher v. Air Force, 96 MSPR 203 (2004)

Charge: Indecent and immoral conduct and sexual harassment. A female coworker of the appellant claimed he touched her buttocks and breast, kissed her, and "slid a wrench up her shorts."

Agency's Penalty: Removal

Judge's Penalty: Reversed the removal.

Board's Penalty: Reinstated the removal. The Board found that the appellant was held to a higher standard of conduct because he was an "informal supervisor" to the 20-year old summer hire coworker and, therefore, occupied a position of trust when he was working with her. The Board also found the appellant's misconduct was serious and repeated and that he was on notice that the agency had a zero-tolerance policy for sexual harassment. His denial of the charges against him revealed a lack of potential for rehabilitation.

Fernandez v. Agriculture, 95 MSPR 63 (2003)

Charge: Improper conduct. Appellant, a compliance officer, submitted a fictitious Activity Report by stating that he had inspected a business on two dates that were subsequent to the closure of the business at that location.

Agency's Penalty: Removal

Judge's Penalty: Reversed the removal. The judge determined that the agency's specification that the appellant had submitted "fictitious" information as opposed to negligent performance of the investigation was "in essence a charge of falsification" that required the agency to establish that the appellant knowingly supplied incorrect information with the intent to defraud, deceive or mislead the agency. The judge then found, however, that the appellant's explanations for his actions rose to the level of negligent performance of his duties rather than intentional falsification and that there was no record evidence that he intended to defraud the agency or that he acted with reckless disregard for the truth. Therefore, the charge failed.

Board's Penalty: Mitigated the removal to a 60-day suspension. The Board found that the judge erred by re-characterizing the charge as "falsification" and thereby requiring the agency to prove intent. Simple negligence was adequate to sustain the charge as it was crafted. However, when considering lack of intent as a mitigating Douglas Factor, the Board concluded that removal was unreasonable based in part on appellant's 29 years of unblemished service and the fact that a compliance officer cannot be held to a higher standard of conduct as can a law enforcement officer or a supervisor.

Gaines v. Air Force, 94 MSPR 527 (2003)

Charge: Inappropriate behavior toward a supervisor. While discussing working mandatory overtime, the appellant became loud, belligerent and confrontational toward his second-level supervisor. When the supervisor radioed for security police to escort the appellant off of the base, the appellant made disparaging remarks about the supervisor.

Agency's Penalty: Removal

Judge's Penalty: Mitigated to a 30-day suspension. The appellant's disrespectful behavior toward the supervisor was not shown to be "either premeditated or done with a purpose to be disrespectful." He also found that the appellant was tired, he was motivated by his feelings of stress and inability to work overtime safely, and "his behavior was an unthinking response to [the] unexpected situation" of being ordered to work overtime. The administrative judge determined further that the only profanity used by the appellant referred to the ambulance driver and not to any supervisor.

Board's Penalty: Reinstated the removal. Although the appellant had 28 years of service, 20 of which were with the agency, he also had four prior disciplinary actions taken for similar misconduct. Disrespectful insolent misconduct directed at a supervisor so seriously undermines the capacity of management to maintain employee discipline that no agency should be expected to exercise forbearance for such conduct more than once.

Gmitro v. Army, 95 MSPR 89 (2003)

Charge: Failing to observe regulations and sleeping on duty after the terrorists attacks of September 11, 2001.

Agency's Penalty: Removal

Judge's Penalty: Mitigated to a 120-day suspension. Although the appellant worked as a police officer at a location within miles of the 9/11 attacks, the judge questioned the agency's established procedures to designate the appropriate threat level after the September 11, 2001 terrorist attacks, questioned other installation security procedures, and concluded that the facility could have been reinforced after those attacks, making the appellant's misconduct less serious.

Board's Penalty: Reinstated the removal. Although there were mitigating factors (13 years of service, lack of prior discipline, satisfactory performance evaluations, and commendations for work as a police officer), these were all considered by the deciding official. The Board will independently weigh the relevant factors only if the deciding official failed to demonstrate that he properly considered any specific, relevant mitigating factors before deciding upon a penalty. In this case, the Board noted that either charge was sufficient to sustain the removal penalty.

Lavette v. USPS, DA-0752-02-0708-I-1 (May 28, 2004)

Charges: Misconduct – Charge 1: Engaging in Conduct Characterized as Sexual Harassment by a Subordinate Employee and in Violation of the Postal Service Policy on Sexual Harassment; and Charge 2: Unsatisfactory Performance – Failure to Comply with Postal Regulations and Rules Regarding the Count, Inspection and Adjustments to the City Routes. The sexual harassment charge involved two incidents of using sexually suggestive language with a female coworker.

Agency's Penalty: Removal

Judge's Penalty: Mitigated to a 90-day suspension. In mitigating the penalty, the judge considered the appellant's 13 years of service with the agency, his emotional condition at the time he engaged in the misconduct, the absence of malice involved in the appellant's misconduct, and the lack of evidence indicating that the appellant's performance was ever anything other than satisfactory. With regard to the appellant's emotional state at the time of his misconduct, the judge relied on the appellant's response to the proposal notice, testimony that his wife underwent surgery recently, and that his one-year old son was hospitalized for pneumonia a short time after even though these claims of medical problems were not documented for the record.

Board's Penalty: Reinstated the removal. The judge rejected as not credible the appellant's testimony regarding his inability to follow route inspection and adjustment procedures. The judge further noted, "that the appellant's demeanor during the hearing seemed somewhat suspicious, or at least raised the possibility that he was trying to hide something. When he testified on a number of the critical points at issue … he seemed overly defensive and was not very persuasive on most of his assertion." The Board found that the record evidence in this case did not demonstrate that the appellant's emotional condition, if any, played a part in his misconduct. The appellant provided no specific explanation as to how the health concerns of his wife and son directly contributed to his inability to conduct the requisite consultations under Charge 2.

Lentine v. Treasury, 94 MSPR 676 (2003)

Charge: Failure to follow a direct order to avoid contact with a female coworker. He sent her an instant message by computer.

Agency's Penalty: Removal

Judge's Penalty: Mitigated to a 90-day suspension. The AJ found that the appellant's 26 years of "superior" discipline-free service with the agency indicated a potential for rehabilitation and that the deciding official had not properly considered this Douglas factor.

Board's Penalty: Reinstated the removal. The appellant had received an order in 1997 not to contact the coworker, and he had received a Letter of Reprimand on August 30, 2000, for contacting the coworker by e-mail that advised him that any other "willful or deliberate contact" would subject him to further discipline, "up to and including removal." The appellant's misconduct two years later was intentional and repeated over a period of years despite explicit instructions to stop and warnings of the consequences of noncompliance. An agency need not wait to discipline an employee until his sexually offensive conduct becomes so pervasive and offensive that it constitutes unlawful discrimination under a hostile work environment theory. Moreover, the appellant has shown no remorse for contacting the employee via instant message and he does not appear to recognize that such contact was inappropriate. Instead, throughout the appeal process the appellant has continued to send correspondence to the Board and the agency that refers to the coworker in a sexually offensive and derogatory manner.

Luongo v. Justice, 95 MSPR 643 (2004)

Charges: (1) Unprofessional Conduct, (2) Conduct Unbecoming a Supervisor; and (3) Inattention to Duty. The first two charges concerned sexual harassment. An employee of a local vendor reported unwanted sexual advances made by the appellant. This generated an investigation which found a number of incidents of sexual harassment of female employees who had been hesitant to come forward. The inattention to duty charge arose when the agency reviewed the appellant's personal e-mail account and found nearly 300 unopened messages in his mailbox, many of which had been sent by other management officials.

Agency's Penalty: Removal

Judge's Penalty: Mitigated to a 14-day suspension. The judge found that the deciding official failed to fully consider all of the relevant mitigating factors in deciding on the penalty. Specifically, the deciding official did not fully consider the appellant's potential for rehabilitation, the environment in which he worked, and the circumstances surrounding the comments he made to other female employees. Over the years the appellant had made remarks of a sexual nature to certain female staff members. However, she found that none of these individuals indicated that they were offended by the remarks, and none who testified ever complained about his conduct. Rather, the judge observed that "most of the individuals who testified for the agency acknowledged that use of sexually suggestive language is commonplace" in the workplace. The judge further observed the appellant's testimony that he had never intended to use such language in an offensive manner. With regard to the appellant's potential for rehabilitation, the judge observed that he had not attempted to escape responsibility for his actions. The judge also found that the agency had never warned the appellant regarding his conduct, even though it contended that he had been engaging in such conduct for a number of years.

Board's Penalty: Reinstated the removal. As a Captain and Supervisory Correctional Officer, the appellant held a law enforcement position only two levels below that of the warden. Moreover, as the incumbent of that position, the appellant was a member of the Executive Staff, which is responsible for establishing policy and making decisions regarding the facility's operation. A higher standard of conduct and a higher degree of trust are required of an incumbent of a position with law enforcement duties. A higher standard of conduct is also required of a supervisor. Consequently, a very high standard of conduct and trust was required of the appellant, who managed supervisory law enforcement officers. The appellant's acts of misconduct were not isolated but were carried out over a period of years. Furthermore, despite his testimony that he was aware that this behavior was inappropriate and violated agency policy, the appellant continued to make improper remarks of a sexual nature to his subordinates and to others. All of the female staff members who gave affidavits in the investigation stated that they found the appellant's comments or conduct to be unwelcome if not offensive.

Negron v. Justice, 95 MSPR 561 (2004)

Charges: (1) Off duty misconduct based on an arrest; (2) Failure to cooperate during an official investigation based on the appellant's refusal to provide the agency with the official documents regarding his arrest; and (3) Providing false information in relation to an official investigation.

Agency's Penalty: Removal

Judge's Penalty: Mitigated to a 60-day suspension. The judge sustained charge 1 (the off-duty misconduct charge), but found that the agency did not prove charges 2 and 3. The judge found that the appropriate penalty for the sustained misconduct was a

60-day suspension. In mitigating the penalty, the judge noted that when an agency's action is based on multiple charges, not all of which are sustained, the Board will independently balance the factors set forth in Douglas.

Board's Penalty: Reinstated the removal. First, the Board reversed the judge and held that charge 2 had been proven. Then, it rejected the judge's proposition that the Board may independently determine an appropriate penalty when fewer than all of the charges are sustained. Instead, the Board stated that where some of the charges are sustained and the agency either indicates that it would have imposed the same penalty based on the sustained charges, or does not indicate to the contrary, the Board's role is not to independently determine the penalty, but to decide whether the agency's choice of penalty is appropriate. The Board cannot "substitute its will" for that of the agency, which is entrusted with managing its workforce. Because the deciding official testified that charge 2 alone was serious enough to warrant removal, the Board set aside the judge's mitigation.

Phillips v. Interior, 95 MSPR 21 (2003)

Charge: Falsification of her 1990 Questionnaire for Sensitive Positions (SF-86). The appellant falsely answered "no" to item 25 on the SF-86, which asked, "Have you ever had a nervous breakdown or have you ever had medical treatment for a mental condition?"

Agency's Penalty: Removal

Judge's Penalty: Sustained the removal

Board's Penalty: Sustained the removal. The agency's table of penalties provides that removal is the only appropriate penalty when an employee makes a falsification "with respect to a material fact or point which would have adversely affected selection for appointment." While there is some question as to whether this particular factual omission would have resulted in having an "adverse effect" on the appellant's appointment, the agency's interpretation of its own regulation in this case is reasonable and entitled to deference.

Quillen v. Treasury, 96 MSPR 154 (2004)

Charges: (1) Misuse of government office equipment, with three supporting specifications; and (2) misuse of official government time.

Agency's Penalty: Removal

Judge's Penalty: Mitigated to a 90-day suspension. The judge found that the appellant's limited use of his government computer to copy his commercial business computer files from one floppy disk to another floppy disk did not constitute sufficient evidence to sustain the agency's third specification in support of its first charge. That specification alleged, in effect, that the appellant had used his government computer for private business purposes after he had received a direct order to cease and desist any such misuse of government property and use of public office for private gain. Because the judge did not sustain all of the agency's specifications in support of its charges, she also reviewed the agency's removal penalty to determine whether it remained within the bounds of reasonableness. The judge found that the agency placed too great a weight on the charged misconduct because the agency did not prove some of the alleged misconduct and it did not present sufficient evidence to support the "magnitude" of some of the misconduct that was proven. The appellant had "absolutely no prior disciplinary incidents of any kind on his record before this action"; he had several years of service with superior or outstanding performance evaluations; and he had a good potential for rehabilitation.

Board's Penalty: Sustained the removal. The misconduct was knowing and intentional, and the misconduct was on-going for an extended period of time. The appellant admitted that he knew that using his government computer for personal business on government time was prohibited, but he did it anyway. He admitted to using government provided internet, e-mail, and telephone service inappropriately for non-work-related purposes, and he admitted to knowingly falsifying his time sheets as a result of his running his private business during work hours, such that he "stole" an estimated $63,000 in salary. Further, the appellant's hearing testimony established that, even after the agency's memorandum ordering him immediately to cease and desist from his misuse of government property and use of public office for private gain, he continued to use his government computer to copy his commercial business files. The appellant's misconduct was serious, intentional, repeated, and directly related to his duties, position, and responsibilities as a Computer Specialist.

Singletary v. Air Force, 94 MSPR 553 (2003)

Charge: Improper receipt of $9,000 in overtime pay.

Agency's Penalty: Removal

Judge's Penalty: Mitigated to a 120-day suspension. The judge decided that the mitigating factors of the appellant's 16 years of discipline-free and successful service and her tearful expression of remorse at the hearing outweighed the aggravating factors in this case.

Board's Penalty: Reinstated the removal. The appellant had 28 separate opportunities over the course of nearly 2 years in which she could and should have brought the overtime overpayments to her agency's attention. Further, when the agency first questioned the appellant about her receipt of the overtime payments, she denied any knowledge of her improper receipt of the payments. The appellant did not actually admit that she received the overtime payments until after the agency had conducted its investigation and had proposed to remove her. Although the Board has found that an appellant's failure to bring a mitigating factor to an agency's attention does not prohibit a judge from considering that factor, the Board has noted that such failure merely affects the weight of the factor. The Board has found that an employee's admission of his misconduct and his expression of remorse are indicative of his rehabilitative potential and constitute a significant mitigating factor when the employee notifies an agency of his wrong doing of his own volition, prior to the agency's initiating an investigation into the misconduct. However, where an employee's admission of misconduct and expression of remorse do not come until after the agency conducts its investigation, the Board has found that the employee's contrition is entitled to little or no mitigating weight.

Thomas v. USPS, CH-0752-03-0559-I-1 (May 25, 2004)

Charge: Unauthorized absence from assignment outside the workplace without authorization, gaining remuneration for work he failed to perform, and illegal drug use.

Agency's Penalty: Removal

Judge's Penalty: Mitigated to a 120-day suspension. The judge concluded that the appellant showed potential for rehabilitation and that the agency relied on uncharged misconduct when selecting a penalty (that the employee had previously purchased and used marijuana on duty while on the agency's premises).

Board's Penalty: Reinstated the removal. It is proper for an agency to rely on uncharged misconduct when selecting a penalty so long as the employee is put on notice of what the agency is considering as was done in this case in the proposal letter.

Tisdell v. Air Force, 94 MSPR 44 (2003)

Charge: Failure to attend mandatory shop refresher training and failure to observe standard safety procedures. Specifically, the agency charged that the appellant arrived late to a scheduled shop refresher training class and was not permitted to attend because the class had already started. The agency also charged that on one occasion the appellant's work stand was not grounded as required during all sanding and painting operations.

Agency's Penalty: Removal

Judge's Penalty: Mitigated to a 45-day suspension. The judge did not sustain the first charge and held that the second charge (failure to abide by safety regulations) did not warrant removal.

Board's Penalty: Reinstated the removal. Within a two year period preceding the charged misconduct, the appellant received a five-day suspension for failure to request leave in accordance with established procedures and failure to follow the directives in a sick leave abuse letter; a five-day suspension for failure to comply with directives outlined in a sick leave abuse letter; a 10-day suspension for unauthorized absences and failure to request leave in accordance with established procedures; and a 30-day suspension for leaving the job without permission. While the administrative judge found that the sustained safety-related charge lacked "significant similarity" to the attendance misconduct for which the appellant received these suspensions, the Board agreed with the agency that the sustained charge represents a continuation of the appellant's repeated failure or refusal to follow agency directives and procedures. This continued disregard of rules and procedures destroyed the trust and confidence his supervisors needed to have in him, and demonstrates that the appellant has little or no potential for rehabilitation.

Magic Words - The principles in these somewhat older cases are still good law. However, more recent cases have given us some good principles as well; in fact, specific language that, if true, you could use verbatim to support a removal:

- Employee's conduct affected management's trust and confidence.
- Serious and intentional misconduct.
- Lost faith in employee's integrity and responsibility.
- Trustworthiness has been called into question.
- Because there was a prior suspension, he has demonstrated he is unwilling or unable to improve his conduct.
- Seriousness of failure to cooperate in investigation caused loss of trust.
- Lack of judgment is particularly serious; could not allow the employee to continue working.
- High level management position with a significant fiduciary responsibility.
- The misconduct compromised management's willingness to trust in his ability to function as a supervisor.
- Seriously compromised management's trust in her ability to function.
- Entirely justified image of untrustworthiness; could not reasonably be expected to function with full effectiveness in a non-supervisory position if demoted.
- The agency had lost trust in the appellant and that trust was an essential requirement in the appellant's position because of his access to the agency's computer network.

Always remember, when it comes to doing a Douglas Factor analysis, go big or go home.

Lessons these cases teach - You may never have to deal with any incidents of misconduct like the charges that were brought in the above cases. However, hopefully you picked up on some general charge/penalty principles from reviewing these cases:

- Cases in which the agency can show progressive discipline have an excellent chance of success.

- Always, always, always relate the harm caused by the misconduct to the agency's core mission whenever you can. Use evidence, not just speculation.
- When the misbehaving employee is a supervisor or in law enforcement, feel free to use high standards of conduct.
- The Board takes certain acts of misconduct very seriously and will sustain a termination for just one or two incidents of misbehaving. For example, remember *Gaines v. Air Force*? The Board said that insolent behavior directed toward a supervisor goes to the heart of the employee-supervisor relationship and that "no agency should be expected to exercise forbearance for such conduct more than once." That means a second incident of a bad-mouthing employee can warrant an immediately proposed removal. Tough stuff, but an important tool for you to use if you so choose.

An Evolving Trend in Penalty Defense

As discussed briefly earlier, beginning in 2010, due to a significant change in Board membership, we began to see a series of decisions being issued that turned a major principle of workplace discipline on its head. Ever since the *Douglas* decision was issued in 1981, one of the penalty selection factors has been the penalties meted out by the deciding official to other employees who had engaged in similar misconduct. All other factors being equal, a deciding official knew that if he had previously suspended an employee for improperly charging $1000 to his government credit card, he could not now remove an employee for the same identical misconduct (without a REALLY good reason). Comparator employees for this purpose had to be in the same chain of command as the current perpetrator and had to be employed in situations "nearly identical" to those of the employee at issue.

In a trilogy of cases issued in 2010, subsequently reinforced in similar lead cases issued in 2011 and 2012, the Board changed that narrow scope of comparator employees from the same "chain of command" to "the agency." Additionally, it specifically rejected the principle that the work situations had to be "nearly identical" and began comparing employees who had engaged in sort-of-similar misconduct from a wide range of locations and disparate types of work. The outcome is that if a terminated employee can point to another employee elsewhere in the agency who has engaged in related misconduct in the past three or four years, and who was not fired, the agency stands a very good chance of having the removal set aside and the employee returned to work.

This is a terrible situation. It is bad for management because it is impossible to know all the other semi-similar misconduct that has occurred everywhere in an agency (remember, we are talking all misconduct, not just disciplined-misconduct). Additionally, it is bad for employees because now managers will choose to remove individuals who might otherwise have received a lesser penalty in order to keep the penalty bar high. For example, if Supervisor Smith is considering selecting a penalty less than removal because he feels sympathy for the employee, he will be told he must go ahead and terminate the employee instead. If he were to choose a lesser penalty, he has now prevented all the other managers in the agency from choosing removal.

This "comparator" trend continues to evolve. The last Board member whose term recently expired had already expressed an understanding of the harm it is causing. The White House issued an executive order in 2018 declaring that agency-wide comparisons for similar misconduct were unnecessary. The difficulty is that we have not yet had a specific rejection or the agency-wide philosophy of the Terrible Trilogy in a precedential MSPB decision. Hopefully, a newly-constituted Board will review this issue and state specifically that a supervisor's selection of a penalty is not restricted to penalties meted out by other supervisors within the agency. Until that time, conservative agencies should consider the following

- Limit the knowledge the deciding official has about other discipline within the agency. The Board has held that a supervisor can make a decision based on his current knowledge, and that he does not have an obligation to investigate the possibility of comparator employees.

- If the employee identifies some agency employee who was not fired for similar misconduct, find some other agency employee who *was indeed fired* for similar misconduct. We have had a single case in which the Board appeared to endorse this approach. One precedential case is better than no precedential cases.
- If you have a particular type of misconduct that you have not fired for before, send out a notice to all employees that you plan to fire for it in the future. Then start firing people. MSPB has specifically endorsed this approach.

Well, that just about covers the basics of disciplining employees for misconduct and removing or demoting them for unacceptable performance. The principles and guidelines we have covered so far should give you a firm foundation in just about any employee accountability situation. However, there are a few situations that are so inherently challenging for the supervisor to handle that we will devote the entire next chapter to discussing strategies for dealing with them should they arise.

Chapter 6
Handling Special Challenges

Discipline and performance challenges can be as varied as the two million-plus individuals who make up the federal workforce. The guidelines and principles discussed in the first several chapters will help you deal with all of them. This chapter will discuss six special situations that might arise, along with recommended strategies for supervisors to successfully defend the discipline and performance actions taken. We'll discuss what you should do when you face one of these special challenges.

Whistleblowers

A whistleblower is someone who publicly divulges an allegation of waste, fraud, or abuse. Congress loves whistleblowers. Congress loves them because the Legislative Branch gives money every year to the Executive Branch (remember high school civics?) and whistleblowers who publicly divulge such waste, fraud, and abuse in the Executive Branch let Congress know when the Executive Branch could be doing a better job with its allowance. As a country, we benefit when one of our citizens risks his personal wellbeing to bring malfeasance into the open. Think of the soldiers who reported the abuse of prisoners in Iraq, or the employee who reported the misplaced headstones at Arlington cemetary. By making the public aware of these acts of misconduct, these whistleblowers helped us to become a better society – while putting themselves at risk.

Because of the high value we place on whistleblowers, Congress has provided extensive protections to federal employees who make public examples of government waste, fraud or abuse. Those protections are especially apparent in the disciplinary process. Whistleblowers historically have been subjected to termination and other discipline for making public disclosures about government mismanagement. When an agency takes disciplinary action against a whistleblower, it has a higher burden of proof to show that the reason for the discipline is not related to the protected disclosure (e.g., the whistleblowing). If you supervise an employee who is a whistleblower, you can still take a disciplinary action against him for misconduct or poor performance – you just have to be more careful in how you go about it, and the action may not be motivated by the fact that the employee blew the whistle.

First, though, you need to know what a person has to do to be considered a whistleblower and get these special protections. For our purposes, a whistleblower is a government employee who discloses:

- A violation of any law, rule, or regulation;
- Gross mismanagement or a gross waste of funds;
- An abuse of authority; or
- A substantial and specific danger to public health or safety.

If the disclosure contains information that by law cannot be revealed to the public (e.g., documents officially classified as "secret," patient medical care records, or taxpayer information), then the disclosure is not protected and the employee is not a whistleblower. Other than these limited exceptions, all other disclosures are covered if they fit into one of the categories above.

It is easy to picture the "classic" whistleblower. He is summoned to appear on Capitol Hill to testify in front of a panel of distinguished Senators or members of Congress. The bright lights go on, the cameras start to roll, and the individual puts his job and sometimes his entire ability to make a living on the line as he responds to pointed questions with disclosures of government waste, fraud, or abuse. Perhaps it is about the $650 Home Depot hammer made famous by Vice President Al Gore, or maybe it is the mistreatment of detainees being held by our operatives overseas. It might be that the disclosure is made on 60 Minutes or in an interview printed in the Washington Post. Whatever the topic may be, the big picture disclosure of "secret" government misdoing in a major public forum is relatively easy to comprehend. It is also relatively rare.

The whistleblower protection law is not limited to protecting only the most public disclosures. It also protects an employee in any of the following situations:

- An employee who complains to the agency's safety officer that the rules regarding designated smoking areas are not being enforced by a particular supervisor.
- An employee who comments at church to a fellow parishioner (who happens to be a management official at the same agency) that another supervisor plans agency-funded business trips every couple of months to visit his daughter who is in college in a town across the country.
- An employee who complains in a letter to a Congresswoman that his supervisor submitted a cab fare to the airport for reimbursement by the agency, even though the supervisor actually got a ride from his sister.

Yes, many employees are defined (and protected) as whistleblowers, and do not even know it. To outsiders, whistleblowers may be seen as whiners, tattletales, or leakers. Under the law, though, they are just as protected as all the other brave citizens who have publicly divulged government misconduct.

Perhaps the most interesting aspect of this broad definition of a whistleblower is this: the facts that are alleged in a disclosure do not have to be true. Even if an employee makes allegations that turn out to be absolutely wrong, the employee is still a whistleblower – as long as he had a good-faith reasonable belief in the truthfulness of his allegations.

Hey, we warned you that Congress loves whistleblowers.

You can still discipline an employee who engages in misconduct or remove an employee who fails a performance Demonstration Period even if he is a whistleblower, but you need to keep three things in mind when you do:

1. Instead of having the burden to prove the fundamental elements of your case by either preponderant (see Chapter Two on misconduct) or substantial (see Chapter Three on performance) evidence, you will have to prove your case by "clear and convincing" evidence, a higher burden of proof that requires more evidence.

2. With rare exception, you cannot discipline a government employee for making the statements that constitute the protected disclosure.

3. If you initiate a disciplinary action against a whistleblower, that employee has the right to seek immediate protection from the Office of Special Counsel (OSC). If OSC concludes that the disciplinary action may be motivated by a desire to reprise against the employee for whistleblowing, it will seek a "stay" of the action from the Merit Systems Protection Board. A stay blocks you from going forward with your action until OSC completes its investigation and makes a final determination.

If OSC concludes that you, the management official who initiated the disciplinary action, were motivated by a desire to reprise against a whistleblower, OSC can prosecute you and have you suspended, demoted, fired, fined, or barred from government service. Although this rarely happens, you do not want to get on OSC's bad side.

In addition to OSC, there are private organizations that provide legal services to whistleblowers. When you have a problem employee who is also a whistleblower, the process to remove the employee and succeed in the appeal is quite a bit more challenging than it would be otherwise.

Recommended tactic – Employees who are whistleblowers can indeed be subjected to discipline, including termination, for non-whistleblowing activities. It might take a little more work but it can be done successfully if you accumulate the level of evidence needed to prove the fundamental elements of the action by a clear and convincing standard. You should also adhere to the following guidelines:

- Have more proof for every element than necessary; do not conclude that you will "get by" on some matter when a little more time and a little more effort will provide you with a solid case on that particular point.

- When confronted, gleefully acknowledge (OK, maybe just a notch below "gleeful") that the employee has the right to make protected disclosures and that you fully support that right; reinforce that the action you are taking has nothing to do with the disclosure and that it is founded in the merits of the case.

- Go out of your way to treat the employee with respect; give every appearance that you are moving forward based on legitimate management reasons – because that is what you are doing.

- Do not say, write, or email anything that would embarrass you if it were printed on the front page of your local newspaper or in the agency's newsletter.

- If contacted by an OSC investigator, do not answer any questions until you have spoken with your agency's employee relations experts or legal counsel. In very serious situations, consider arranging for consultation with a private attorney who specializes in federal employment law.

Most importantly, never initiate or otherwise participate as a management official in a termination action designed to rid the government of an employee because he is a whistleblower. Not only would that be against the law, but you would make Congress very unhappy.

EEO Complaints

Several years ago, a senior official who had accepted an early-out retirement remarked to a reporter that he was glad to get out of a leadership in government because it was "no longer fun to manage since the discrimination complaint process had constipated the personnel system." Well, we may not necessarily agree with his assessment, but that is an accurate description of how a lot of supervisors feel.

Federal employees have the legal right to file Equal Employment Opportunity (EEO) complaints regarding any perceived injustice. An employee needs only to make contact with an EEO Counselor and fill out a short form that accuses a supervisor of being motivated by one of the protected classes that the civil rights laws define, and a multi-stage investigation is commenced.

The protected EEO classes are:

- Race
- Color
- National Origin
- Religion
- Sex
- Age
- Disability
- Genetic information
- Reprisal for prior EEO activity

No proof is necessary to initiate the EEO complaint process. If the employee chooses to file a formal complaint and there's evidence that, if true, could permit an inference of discrimination, then a formal investigation is launched. Trained professional investigators interview the supervisor and perhaps others in the workplace regarding the allegations of discrimination. Supervisors and other management officials can be required to produce documents, testimony and other evidence to try to establish that they acted without discriminatory animus.

After the investigations are over and both the employee and the agency have responded to the facts unearthed, the employee can request a hearing before the Equal Employment Opportunity Commission (EEOC), where the agency defends itself against the discrimination complaint. Hearings come complete with witnesses and lawyers and judges to resolve the matter alleged in the complaint. All this can happen without the employee having to do much more than articulate a reasonable claim of discriminatory treatment.

And it's all free. Free, at least, as far as the employee is concerned. He, of course, can hire a lawyer to help him present his case, but legal assistance (and legal expense) is not required. Our system guarantees the employee a right to have his case investigated and a right to have his arguments heard before an impartial administrative judge without necessarily spending a dime.

In addition, the employee also enjoys legal protection from retribution from the agency for filing the discrimination complaint in the first place. Such retribution is commonly referred to as EEO reprisal or retaliation. Every seasoned practitioner can identify at least one case in which there was a finding of no discrimination on the merits of the employee's initial discrimination complaint (for example, race or age discrimination), and then a finding of discrimination because of the reprisal actions the agency took after the first complaint was filed. Because the federal government's discrimination complaint process can be a very powerful weapon in the hands of an employee who believes he has been treated unjustly, some supervisors will ignore or choose not to act on misconduct or poor performance if the employee is someone who the supervisor perceives is likely to file a discrimination complaint.

> *I know that she doesn't do a lick of work, is at least 20 minutes late every day, and that she's mean and nasty to everyone she meets. But what am I supposed to do? She's the only [fill in the blank with the protected category of your choice] in the office.*

> *Fire him during probation? Man, I would love to. He's insolent, lazy, disobedient, and he uses profanity to excess. Unfortunately, he's also [here's*

another blank to fill in] and I just know he would file a complaint against me.

Well, for those of you out there who are afraid to take a disciplinary or performance action against an employee because of their protected status, we have a single memorable piece of life-changing advice for you:

GET OVER IT!

Life is not guaranteed to be just and fair all the time, and sometimes the better approach is to prepare for the inevitable rather than try to avoid it by inaction.

Maybe you don't like the discrimination complaint system. Well, like it or not, if you're a federal supervisor, it's what you have to work with. The elimination of improper workplace discrimination is a top priority for Congress and the EEO complaint process is the result of the Congressional attempt to eliminate discriminatory employment practices wherever they exist. If you are ever the victim of discrimination, you will be very happy that such a system is in place to protect you from abuse.

One additional note: While we could all agree that many discrimination complaints seem to be frivolous, these laws exist to protect people from illegal discrimination. When discrimination occurs, it is a terrible thing. A person's sex, race, age, and religion (and every other protected class) is at the core of his identity, and being discriminated against because of that very personal thing can cause severe lifelong psychological or physical injury. The system is set up to try to protect people from these types of injuries.

Recommended tactic – If you have a problem employee who you think may invoke the federal EEO complaint process, here's how to proceed:

- Commit to treating this employee just like you would any other problem employee. Treating someone with more leniency because he is likely to file a discrimination complaint is about as bad a decision as a government supervisor can make. Accept that discrimination complaints may come and be prepared to defend your actions when they do. Federal supervisors, on average, will receive two discrimination complaints against them during their federal service. In most cases, no discrimination is found. So, don't be afraid of an EEO complaint.

- Move quickly and directly to initiate either progressive discipline or the unacceptable performance procedures with the problem employee. Have the necessary letters drafted and issued as expediently as possible. Be ready for settlement proposals to be developed as a result of the EEO complaint process, and work with your management support staff to come up with options that allow you to correct errant conduct or performance while reaching a resolution of the complaint.

- Be prepared to back up your decisions with full documentation. If you are accused of illegal discrimination, deny it calmly but with conviction. Try to keep your emotions out of it. As personally offensive as it may feel to be called a racist or sexist or some other [fill in the blank]-ist, you do little for your defense by losing your temper or disparaging the accuser.

- Do not allow the EEO complaint process to derail your discipline or performance actions. Deal with the counselors and investigators in the normal course of business while keeping up the offensive about continued misconduct and poor performance.

- Be careful what you say. A lot of words and actions can be given an unintended meaning when viewed within the crucible of an EEO investigation. A reference to "you people" may be intended to refer to the entire clerical staff, but it will sound like it is being applied to a protected class of people when the employee's attorney brings it up in an EEOC hearing.

The main tactic for dealing with an employee who might file a discrimination complaint is to accept this reality and prepare to deal with it as you continue to do the job you are being paid to do: maintain productivity and effectiveness in a government workplace utilizing supervisory skills and tools to help fulfill your agency's mission. You may be able to avoid an EEO complaint by taking no action when it is needed, but you will be dishonoring the position of leadership to which you have been appointed. Accept that the EEO complaint process is part of the price we pay for a free society, recognize that the situation is not going to get better unless you do something about it, and then move ahead with the assistance of management support staff. It will not be enjoyable and some of it will be difficult, but by following the procedures we have laid out in this book and by making decisions based on business reasons (not a protected EEO class), you will be successful.

Just do it.

Union Officials

On occasion, a supervisor will refrain from disciplining an employee because that employee is a union official. If the employee is active in the union, you can certainly expect the union to vigorously defend him from discipline. But employees who are union officials should be held to the same performance and conduct standards as all other employees. So, if your misbehaving employee happens to be a union official, you can proceed with progressive discipline or an unacceptable performance action as you would any other employee, with the following caveats:

First, it is illegal to discipline an employee solely because he is a union official and he represents the interests of fellow employees. To do so would be a prohibited personnel practice and could result in a disciplinary action (including termination) against you as the offending supervisor, and any management support staff who assisted in implementing the improper action.

Second, the courts have recognized that an employee acting in the role of a union official may sometimes act in a manner that would not be tolerated from the same employee who was simply performing his regular job functions. For example, if an employee and his supervisor engage in a loud, heated discussion about a work matter, and the employee terminates the meeting by walking out of the supervisor's office and slamming the door hard behind him, the supervisor might well be within his rights to reprimand or even suspend the employee for a first offense of disrespectful conduct. On the other hand, if that employee is engaged in the same sort of loud, heated discussion with the same supervisor, and the subject of the discussion is directly related to the employee's role as a union official, management has to refrain from disciplining and be more tolerant of conduct that might be characterized as "robust debate" or simply forceful representation of the interests of the bargaining unit.

Of course, there is an outside limit to this "robust debate" concept, and it varies depending on each specific situation. We know that if our union official employee in the above example were to strike his supervisor during the course of defending a bargaining unit principle, that employee certainly could be disciplined in spite of his union status. The difficult part is that most situations fall somewhere between the union official slamming the door and knocking the supervisor to the ground. That's why the best strategy in these situations involves more than just the immediate supervisor.

Recommended tactic – When confronted with misconduct or unacceptable performance from an employee who is a union official:

- First, decide whether the misconduct or performance problem is due to the employee's union duties. If it is, immediately contact your labor relations staff for guidance about how to proceed. When disciplining union officials, there are a lot of factors beyond the scope and immediate concern of the employee's supervisor. For example, if that individual is heavily involved in an important bargaining situation that might have an impact throughout the agency, then the better course of action for the immediate supervisor may be to postpone the misconduct/performance action, at least until the bargaining is completed. We don't like that this big picture approach sometimes arises, but the overall benefit and harm to the organization may need to be determined at a relatively high level when you're thinking of disciplining a union official.

- If the misconduct/performance problem is NOT a result of the employee's union duties, proceed as you would with a non-union employee, but with a good measure of extra care. Disciplining employees who are union officials will draw significant interest from the union (maybe even at a national level) and are subject to investigation by the U.S. Office of Special Counsel and the Federal Labor Relations Authority. You want to be sure that you have very good explanations for everything you do, and good documentation to back up every action you take.
- Even when the problem obviously flows from non-union duties, coordinate early and often with your labor relations staff. Their expertise will be invaluable when it comes to considering the big picture, and they will be able to help focus your actions on the non-union duties of the employee (for example, helping you distinguish time spent as "official time" on representational work from time you might otherwise have expected the employee to be performing his officially assigned duties).

Disciplining a union official is not something that any supervisor looks forward to. However, if done carefully and thoughtfully (keeping the case law in mind) it will be possible to implement appropriate discipline where it is warranted.

Leave Abusers

A significant number of the 10,000+ federal employees who are fired each year are fired based at least in part on a charge of leave abuse. That does not necessarily mean that the most common act of misconduct in government is leave abuse, it just means that is one of the most frequent charges used. That is because leave abuse is relatively easy to prove (the employee is either at work, or not), and because employees who engage in other types of misconduct often also engage in leave abuse. Because it happens so often, it's important to know how to deal with it.

Leave abuse cases can get complicated because of the variety of leave types available to employees. Agencies sometimes develop slack procedures for dealing with routine leave use, an informality that can be a problem when abuse develops. First, let's take a look at the main forms of leave that we see in disciplinary situations:

1. **Annual leave** – Federal employees earn annual leave at the rate of four to eight hours per pay period, depending on length of service. Annual leave can be used for anything from periodic vacations from work to short periods of personal time. Interestingly, although employees earn annual leave as a right, there is no regulation or law that requires a supervisor to actually grant the use of that leave. Theoretically, a supervisor could refuse to grant an employee's request for accumulated annual leave until the employee started to lose annual leave due to the 240-hour cap on the maximum amount of leave that can be carried over from one leave year to the next. That's never done, of course, but it does highlight the importance of the supervisor's control over whether and when annual leave can be granted.
2. **Sick leave** – Federal employees earn sick leave at the rate of four hours per pay period regardless of length of service, and there is no cap on sick leave accumulation. Supervisors do not decide whether to grant sick leave; employees have a right to take accrued sick leave if they are indeed incapacitated for duty due to illness, disease, or injury. In addition to using sick leave for personal incapacitation and medical examinations, an employee may also use sick leave for care of a sick family member, or for bereavement, adoption, or organ donation.
3. **Leave without pay** – LWOP is employee placement into a non-work/non-pay status at the employee's request. Although there is no limit to how long an employee can remain on LWOP, as a practical matter, anything over six months begins to affect payment for health benefits and credit for retirement. With a couple of major exceptions, employees do not have an entitlement to LWOP.

4. **Administrative leave** – Sometimes an agency will direct or allow an employee to be in a non-work status while being paid a regular salary. There is a statutory 10-day limit to the amount of administrative leave an employee can legally be granted each year.
5. **Notice Leave** – This relatively new category of leave allows the employee to be placed in a non-work status while being paid, for the duration of the 30-day notice period after a removal has been proposed, if the agency can show that leaving the employee at work jeopardizes a legitimate government interest.
6. **Investigative Leave** - Also a relatively new leave category, this is a form of paid absence that an agency can use to remove an employee from the workplace during the pendency of an agency investigation into suspected employee misconduct. Investigative leave can be used by the agency in 30-day increments, up to a total of 90 days.
7. **Absence without leave** – Although not a true leave category, AWOL certainly comes up in disciplinary situations, and can be the basis for removal if it is extensive or repeated. An employee is AWOL when he is absent from work and the absence has not been approved. Employees in AWOL status are not paid.

Now that we have described the basic types of leave, let's discuss the details of common problems encountered in each leave category.

Annual leave – Some employees carry the maximum amount of annual leave in their accounts; others keep their leave account balances at or near zero. Neither of these is a problem so long as the organization's workflow is not disrupted. However, leave use does become a problem when it is routinely unplanned for and requires significant last-minute maneuvering of staff and resources to accommodate the leave request. There are several things to keep in mind when you are dealing with an employee who has an annual leave problem:

- Employees do not take annual leave. Annual leave is requested and then approved. Problem employees who say, "Put me on leave for tomorrow" (or worse yet, "Put me on leave for yesterday") should be reminded that they have no entitlement to take annual leave tomorrow or any other day regardless of the amount of annual leave in their account, and that their request that can be denied or approved by the supervisor based on the legitimate needs of the workplace.

- All agencies have policies that require annual leave be requested and approved in advance except in "emergency" situations. If a problem employee calls in one morning claiming an emergency and requesting annual leave for the day, if you have any doubts about the legitimacy of the claim, decline to approve the request over the phone. Instead, tell the employee that you will discuss his leave status with him once he returns to work. Then, you can listen to his story, request any evidence of his claim that you feel is necessary, and decide whether to grant the request. This is much better than approving the request over the phone and trying to disapprove the request retroactively when the employee returns to work.
- A supervisor can discipline an employee who does not follow leave proper leave request procedures even if the annual leave is eventually approved. This is also true for sick leave and LWOP.
- You are within your rights as a supervisor to ask an employee to explain or document a request for unplanned annual leave, and base your approval or disapproval on the reason. For example, it would be reasonable for you to grant a request for annual leave if the employee states he needs it because he has to appear in court on a personal matter, and to disapprove it if he wants the time to attend an afternoon baseball game. An employee has a right not to tell you why he is requesting annual leave, but you have the right to deny the request if the employee refuses to tell you the reason for the request.
- As a general rule, an employee cannot be disciplined for using approved leave. If you approve a leave request, you cannot turn around and reprimand, suspend, or terminate the employee for using the leave. However, there is one unusual situation in which an employee can be terminated for being on approved leave for an

extended period of time, and we will discuss that situation in the following section on sick leave abuse.

Sick leave – Compared to the private sector, government agencies are relatively generous with the accumulation and use of sick leave. Many senior employees who have accrued hundreds or thousands of hours of sick leave see their sick leave account as a form of disability insurance should they become medically restricted from performing their jobs. Supervisors are required by regulation to grant sick leave to a federal employee who:

- Receives medical, dental, or optical examination or treatment;
- Is incapacitated for the performance of duties by physical or mental illness, injury, pregnancy, or childbirth;
- Provides care for a family member who is incapacitated by a medical or mental condition or attends to a family member receiving medical, dental, or optical examination or treatment;
- Provides care for a family member with a serious health condition;
- Makes arrangements necessitated by the death of a family member or attends the funeral of a family member;
- Would, as determined by the health authorities having jurisdiction or by a health care provider, jeopardize the health of others by his or her presence on the job because of exposure to a communicable disease; or
- Must be absent from duty for purposes relating to the adoption of a child, including appointments with adoption agencies, social workers, and attorneys, court proceedings, required travel, and any other activities necessary to allow the adoption to proceed.

The problem develops when employees continually use their sick leave at inopportune times and in manners that suggest they may really not be sick. Here are some things to keep in mind:

- You can require an employee to bring in medical documentation as evidence of how sick he is. Usually before doing this, an agency will issue the employee a "Leave Restriction" letter that specifies in detail what the employee must do to obtain your approval of his leave request, and what documentation he must present from his physician as evidence of his incapacity. For example, the supervisor might require that a request for sick leave be accompanied by the following information from the employee's physician:

1. The history of the medical condition including summaries of findings from previous examinations, treatment, and responses to treatment;
2. Clinical findings from the most recent medical evaluation including any of the following which have been obtained: results of physical examinations, laboratory tests, x-rays, EKGs, and other diagnostic procedures;
3. Diagnosis;
4. Prognosis, including plans or recommendations for future treatment and an estimate of the expected date of full or partial recovery; and
5. An explanation of how the employee's medical condition impacts overall health and activities, including the basis for a conclusion that restrictions, accommodations, or leave are warranted.

- Medical information can be tricky, so be thoughtful when making requests for medical documentation and discuss what you need with your HR department, as they may be the department to actually collect the medical information. Oftentimes supervisors inadvertently come across medical information beyond what was requested, make decisions based on that information and unknowingly violate employee rights under the Americans with Disabilities Act and the Rehabilitation Act. A general rule is to gather the least amount of medical information necessary to make a determination about whether to grant sick leave. If this seems contradictory to you, you're correct – there are some differences between what medical information OPM says supervisors may gather and what the EEOC has said is appropriate. Remember again, you are not alone, and you have agency resources to help you know how to approach this type of situation.

- It is the employee's responsibility to present medical evidence to support the sick leave request to the supervisor, not the supervisor's responsibility to go out and get the evidence. Tell the employee in detail what evidence you need, and then deny the leave request if the medical evidence presented by the employee is inadequate. Do not make the mistake of trying to deal directly with the employee's physician yourself.
- If the employee brings you equivocal medical evidence and you do not want to outright deny the request, you can offer that the employee be examined at agency expense by a physician of your choosing. This is an option you can offer the employee, but cannot order. The old days of being able to direct an employee under threat of discipline to undergo a "fitness for duty" examination are long gone (except in the case of established physical or mental standards for the specific position occupied).
- Although an employee is entitled to use sick leave for a medical or dental treatment, the supervisor retains the authority to approve when sick leave for that purpose will be taken. For example, if an employee requests sick leave for a routine dental cleaning on the day that you expect your heaviest workload for the month, you are perfectly within your rights to deny the request for that date and to give the employee alternative dates on which you are willing to grant the sick leave request.
- There is no legal entitlement to advanced leave. Advanced sick or annual leave is sometimes extended by the agency beyond what has accrued in the employee's leave account, so that a leave "debt" is created. Although you may choose to grant advanced leave to a good employee within your agency's leave policy, you may decide not to exercise your discretion to do so with a problem employee.
- The U.S. Supreme Court has made it clear that there is a large difference between an employee who is medically restricted and an employee who has a disability and is legally entitled to reasonable accommodation. If an employee tells you he can no longer do his job because of some medical problem and asks that you change his job in some way to accommodate his medical problem, you need to immediately check with your reasonable accommodation

coordinator to determine whether you have an obligation to grant the request, or whether you can (and perhaps should) deny it. For example, if an employee provides a medical report that concludes the employee's supervisor is causing so much stress the employee just cannot come to work, the employee is probably not disabled, is not entitled to accommodation, and may be looking for a new job if he doesn't find a quick cure. If you want to play hardball, here is how this could work:

1. Law enforcement officer: "Boss, my doctor says that I can't do this work anymore. It's too hot out here in the sun, all the dust and exhaust fumes are bad for my lungs, and the stress of dealing with hundreds of nasty people every day is causing me to be depressed, lose sleep, lose my appetite, and suffer from post-traumatic stress disorder. If you would just reassign me to an inside air-conditioned job on the day shift with no weekend work, I would be just fine."
2. Response of well-prepared supervisor: "Gee, I'm really sorry to hear about your medical problems. It would be helpful if you could get your physician to write all of this up in a medical report that describes in detail your multiple problems."
3. Law enforcement officer: [Trots off to see Dr. Crackpot, a family friend who will write down anything for his old buddy, for a price. The employee then delivers the doctor's report to the supervisor.]
4. Well-prepared supervisor: [Walks over to the expert employee relations staff which quickly prepares a letter proposing the employee's termination for medical inability to perform, based on the employee's own medical evidence.]

Whoa! Could it really be this easy? Oh, yes – yes it can. Unless an employee meets the definition of a qualified individual with a disability (which may be the case in the above scenario; you'd want to contact the reasonable accommodation coordinator before step 4), he has to either do the job you assign him or find another job. Of course, if you want to give him that cushy air-conditioned day job, you may. Just remember, you don't have to. For what it is worth, employees terminated for medical inability to perform have good grounds on which to file for disability retirement from the government if they meet the minimum criteria. However, approval of that is a separate matter and is not necessarily your concern as far as the termination itself goes.

Be prepared to contact a news outlet or medical journal to report the medical miracle once the employee realizes that he can be fired for refusing to work due to a purported medical condition. This approach works remarkably well in many situations.

Although approved leave usually is not grounds for discipline, an employee still can be removed if the amount of leave being used is extensive, is due to the employee's medical condition, and there is no foreseeable end in sight to the absence. In a removal of this type, the charge is most often "Unavailability for Work." Usually in this situation, the employee begins requesting sick and annual leave because of some chronic illness or injury. Then, once the leave banks are exhausted, the supervisor might agree to approve a request for leave without pay for many weeks or months, expecting (and perhaps hoping) that the employee will eventually recover and be able to return to work. As all of this leave is approved, normally an adverse action would not be appropriate. However, an employee in this situation can be terminated if the following conditions are met:

- *The absences have been for an extended unreasonable period of time, and the employee was absent for compelling reasons beyond his control, so that agency approval or disapproval of leave was immaterial because the employee could not be on the job.*

  Unfortunately, there is no bright line regulation that states what constitutes a minimum period of absence before a separation action for unavailability can be initiated. The case law suggests that a continual absence of six months straight may be enough time. Alternatively, if the employee's absences are not days in a row, but are intermittent, an action probably can be initiated once the absences total a majority of the work time for the year. The longer the period of accrued absences, the more likely it is that the period will be considered adequate.

- *The available medical evidence suggests that there is no end (or that it is not possible to predict an end) to a need for these absences, and that the agency needs someone in the position on a regular basis.*

  The principle here is that the approval or disapproval of the employee's request for approved leave is immaterial to the employee's presence at the work place; i.e., regardless of whether the leave request is approved or disapproved, the employee will not be able to report to work due to a medical condition. Sometimes the agency will have adequate medical proof in its possession to establish that the employee's return to work cannot be predicted. Other times, it will have very little evidence at all. In either case, prior to termination the employee should be given a chance to present additional evidence by being put on notice that his absence will no longer be tolerated.

- *The employee is put on notice that continued absence will result in removal unless he becomes available for regular full-time employment (or regular part-time employment if the agency's need is only part-time).*

  An employee who has been on approved leave for an extended period of time is justified in believing that the approved leave status will continue unless he is told otherwise. The supervisor lets the employee know that the approval for his absences is about to come to an end by putting the employee on notice. The easiest way to do this is to send a letter to the employee saying that approval for future absences will be discontinued at some specific date in the future (two weeks is a good suggestion) and that the employee will be terminated based on unavailability for work unless he reports for duty by that specific date. The employee should be notified that if he believes his medical condition is going to improve, he must submit medical documentation about his prognosis to establish when he can be expected to return to work. If the employee fails to return to work by the date specified in the letter, or fails to otherwise convince the supervisor that his return is imminent, then approved leave should be discontinued, the employee should be charged AWOL, and his termination should be proposed once the AWOL has exceeded one week. An AWOL charge isn't absolutely necessary, but it adds an extra level of protection for the supervisor should there be some deficiency in another part of the case. Unavailability for work removals are a bit risky and should be avoided if possible. The proactive way to handle an employee who has exhausted his leave bank and is requesting further approved leave is to be very stingy in approving requests for LWOP unless you are very certain that the employee will recover and the employee is a valuable asset to the agency. In a few situations, you will be required to grant approved leave to be in compliance with the Family and Medical Leave Act, the Office of Workers Compensation regulations, or some other regulation that applies to a specific category of absence. Outside these exceptions, the best way to deal with an employee who has used so much leave that his balances are at zero is to decline to approve additional leave unless you have a VERY good reason. If the employee continues to be absent, the supervisor should charge him AWOL and pursue an appropriate level of discipline.

LWOP – As you may have gathered from the discussion above, leave without pay is an approved pay status and, in most situations, cannot be the basis for a disciplinary action. Although an employee is entitled to take sick leave when sick, and although agencies as a matter policy routinely allow employees to take accrued annual leave each year, there are few entitlements to take LWOP or agency policies favoring the grant of such leave. An employee in LWOP status is not at work but is occupying a position that could be filled by another individual who would be available to work. An absent employee costs the agency money for health benefits (among a few other minor expenses) for absences up to six months in length.

LWOP in principle is requested by the employee and granted by the supervisor. A supervisor cannot place an employee on LWOP against the employee's will, and there should be no reason for him to want to do that. If an employee is absent from work and has failed to request leave or has exhausted his leave account, then the careful supervisor will carry the employee in AWOL status. AWOL is not necessarily a reason for the employee to be disciplined, and a supervisor can carry an employee AWOL indefinitely without terminating him (there are cases in which employees have been carried AWOL for a year or more). AWOL can always be retroactively converted to approved leave if future circumstances warrant. It is much more difficult to retroactively convert approved leave to AWOL (as discussed previously).

Administrative leave – Administrative leave is a full pay status during which the employee is not required to work. It is the most unusual category of leave of all because the agency receives so little benefit from the absence, and at a considerable expense. Under the Administrative Leave Act of 2016, this leave is limited to 10 days per year. An experienced supervisor might consider placing an employee on administrative leave if the employee's presence in the workplace could be disruptive and the risk or time involved in suspending the employee without pay puts the supervisor in a difficult situation. Supervisors should consider placing an employee on administrative leave in the following situations:

- There has been a disruptive incident at the workplace and sending the employee home on administrative leave will give him a chance to calm down.
- The employee is willing to trade something of value to the supervisor in exchange for placement on administrative leave.

Notice leave – This category of leave, created under the Administrative Leave Act of 2016, allows agencies to send employees home in a full pay status without requiring the employee to perform work. This type of leave is reserved for the 30-day notice period after an employee has received proposed discipline, most often a proposed termination. In order to use this leave category, the agency has the burden:

1. To show that retaining the employee at work jeopardizes a government interest;
2. To show it considered reassignment;
3. To inform the employee in the proposal; and
4. To keep a record.

It makes sense, in every case of proposed removal, to use this category of leave. At best, the employee who has received news of a proposed removal will be upset and unproductive; at worst the employee might become violent. Don't try to predict the employee's reaction – get the employee out of the workplace immediately on notice leave.

Recommended tactic – The best way to deal with leave problems is to be very conscious of the bright line between situations in which an employee is *entitled* to have leave granted and situations in which the supervisor has the *option* of granting leave. Once that is done, the supervisor should begin to exercise the option of declining to approve leave requests in which there is no employee entitlement, and thereby carrying the employee in AWOL status for the days of absence. Finally, as in most misconduct situations, the supervisor should act promptly to impose discipline for each incident of AWOL. First, a Letter of Reprimand, then a short suspension or a Reprimand in Lieu of Suspension, and then proceed with initiating the eventual termination.

During the process of progressive discipline, keep the onus on the employee to prove any claimed excuses for his absences. If he says he's too sick to work and has no sick leave, give him the opportunity to present you with medical evidence of his limitations and his prognosis. That won't necessarily guarantee an excused absence, but it may affect the penalty selection. Never accept an excuse without being satisfied by evidence that the excuse is legitimate, and remember that even with an excuse, discipline can still be taken.

FMLA – Federal employee entitlements to approved leave under the Family and Medical Leave Act of 1993 (FMLA), *The Federal Employee Family Friendly Leave Act of 1994* (FEFFLA), and Presidential Executive Orders and Memoranda are fraught with complexities and limitations beyond the scope of this text. Rely on your expert management advisers in employee relations to advice you on a case-by-case basis while keeping two bits of good news in mind:

1. The responsibility is usually placed on the employee to specifically invoke a particular right to approved leave prior to the supervisor having the obligation to grant the request, and
2. The supervisor can require the employee to present evidence of the need for the leave. Typically, this request for evidence will be in the form of a request for a written medical certification from the employee's physician that includes:

    a. The date the serious health condition commenced;
    b. The probable duration of the serious health condition, or a specification that the serious health condition is a chronic or continuing condition with an unknown duration; whether the patient is presently incapacitated, and the likely duration and frequency of episodes of incapacity;
    c. The appropriate medical facts within the health care provider's knowledge regarding the serious health condition, including a general statement about the incapacitation, examination, or treatment that may be required;
    d. If the FMLA request is to care for a parent, child, or spouse, the supervisor can demand additional statements from the employee's physician and the employee's relative about the need for the employee's services as a care provider.

Finally, in some fashion or another, encourage the employee who is chronically absent from work to consider resigning and taking care of his personal problems rather than being terminated for misconduct. Explain to the employee that if he resigns with a clean record, it will be much easier to obtain re-employment with a government agency than if he has to report a termination on his next application for employment. The exact way to do this will vary from one situation to the next, but you benefit yourself and perhaps the employee if you help him understand that it might be better for everyone if he took off some time to get his life in order. This approach doesn't work all the time, but when it does, it is a wonderful option to the riskier labor-intensive adverse action process.

Medical Problems

Employees with medical problems often have leave problems. Much of the discussion above relative to dealing with leave problems is applicable when dealing with employees who have medical problems. However, medical issues frequently go beyond absences from work, so we need to discuss those issues in further detail.

Sympathetic situation – We've all been sick at one time or another; sometimes we've been terribly ill. It's completely understandable that we would have sympathy when one of our employees reports that he is too ill to work. However, there is a point at which the supervisor has to maintain sympathy while working to fulfill the agency's mission, and has to remove the employee from government service if the medical condition prevents the employee from performing at an acceptable level. Once that point is reached, it is imperative that the supervisor stick to progressive discipline or the problem will get no better (and will probably get worse).

Disabilities and reasonable accommodation – There is a widespread belief that a government agency has the legal responsibility to accommodate an employee with medical limitations. That belief is wrong. The government's obligation is to reasonably accommodate an employee with medical limitations IF (and only IF) the employee's medical condition rises to the level of a "disability," and the disability can be accommodated without causing the agency an undue hardship.

Here's what the agency is obligated to do for a qualified individual with a disability who has requested reasonable accommodation:

1. Look for a reasonable accommodation that will allow the employee to perform the essential functions of his job without causing an undue hardship.
2. If an accommodation is not possible, look for a vacant, funded position for which he is qualified, at his current grade level. This search must be done up to the department level, world-wide.
3. If there is no vacant, funded position at his grade level, you should look for a vacant, funded position at a lower grade level.
4. If there is nothing available or the employee refuses the reassignment, you can remove the employee for medical inability to perform.

The above is the reasonable accommodation process. Now let's get into the details.

The term "disability" is defined as:

> *A physical or mental impairment that substantially limits one or more of the major life activities of such individual.*

Although succinctly stated, these 19 words have resulted in mountains of litigation and court decisions. The following principles extracted from those decisions should be helpful.

Not all individuals with medical problems meet the definition of individuals with disabilities – but more individuals have disabilities today than did in 2008. When the federal government first started requiring accommodation of individuals with disabilities in the '70s, the threshold to be considered "handicapped" (a now disfavored term) was very low. Alcoholics, drug users, sexual deviants – all were considered to be disabled and entitled to reasonable accommodation of their medical limitations. When it came to disciplining for misconduct, some courts were going so far as to order that agencies forego disciplining disabled employees simply because they were disabled. Practitioners who have been around a long time will remember how alcoholic employees essentially were given a "free bite" at the apple and could only be given a "firm choice" between discipline and getting treatment for their first incident of misconduct.

The Americans with Disabilities Act (ADA) was passed in 1990 with the intent to protect individuals with disabilities from illegal discrimination. Before too long, agencies started spending too much time arguing about whether an employee had a disability, and not enough time determining whether the individual could be reasonably accommodated in his job. Congress dealt with this by passing the Americans with Disabilities Act Amendments Act (ADAAA), which became effective January 1, 2009. The ADAAA shifted the focus from whether a medical condition was bad enough qualify as a disability, to whether the agency has fulfilled its obligations to accommodate the employee.

The ADAAA essentially increased the number of individuals who have disabilities by expanding the definition of "major life activities" and changing the definition of "substantial limitation" to a lower threshold. Congress said the question of whether an individual has a disability should not demand extensive analysis.

In order to receive accommodation, an employee who has a disability must be a qualified individual. The term "qualified" means that he has the required skill, experience, education and other job-related requirements of the position and can also perform the essential functions of the position, with or without reasonable accommodation, and without endangering himself or others.

The good news for most supervisors is that most of your employees with disabilities are able to perform all of the essential functions of their positions without accommodation, or with simple accommodations. You might never even know your employee has a disability. This book is not about those easy situations, though; this book is about problem situations.

Consider the following examples:

An employee with a temporary medical limitation is not disabled and is therefore not entitled to accommodation. The employee with a broken leg or the flu, no matter how debilitating the injury or illness may be, is not entitled to accommodation because his limitation is short-term, and he will recover. He is not an individual with a disability. There are some gray areas of the law when considering conditions that are expected to last for a few months or more, but are still temporary. However, for the most part when you have an employee with a medical problem which time will heal, you do not have an employee with a disability and therefore the employee is not entitled to reasonable accommodation.

An employee who has a medical condition that prevents him from doing just one job might not have a disability. Classic example: The employee brings in irrefutable medical evidence that his supervisor drives him crazy, causes unremitting anxiety and depression, and just generally exacerbates the employee's various medical infirmities to the point that the employee cannot come to work. It is clear that the employee could work for any of a dozen or so other supervisors without a problem, and the agency has vacancies all over the place for which the employee is qualified. Well, it may be a good management practice to reassign the employee to another supervisor, but there is no entitlement to reassignment as a reasonable accommodation of a disability because this is not a disability! An employee who cannot work for a single supervisor, but who can work in other similar jobs under other supervisors, is not prevented by a medical condition from working in a "class" of jobs. Therefore, he can be removed for medical inability to perform.

The agency, and not the employee, selects the reasonable accommodation. The agency is required to discuss accommodation options with the employee. This is called the "interactive process," and the agency ultimately chooses the accommodation among the available options. Suppose an employee has a medical condition that meets the definition of disability, such as epilepsy. Suppose the accommodation that will allow the employee to function is that he work near co-workers who can respond to his aid should he have a seizure at work. The employee currently works an undesirable night shift and asks that the agency accommodate his disability by reassigning him to the cushy day shift where there are lots of co-workers to help should he have a seizure. The agency is perfectly within its rights to decline that request and to assign the employee to a different physical location where other night shift employees are available while retaining him on the 11:00 PM to 7:30 AM work schedule. The employee might well prefer to work days. However, if the agency's accommodation is otherwise reasonable and allows the employee to work within his medical restrictions, then it is free to implement its choice of accommodation.

Employees with disabilities are entitled to modifications to their current job to accommodate their disability. The essential functions of the job should not be changed, but minor modifications (such as providing an ergonomic workstation, a modification of work schedule, or a change in minor job duties) may be appropriate. The supervisor should not lower a performance standard as an accommodation, and is not required to create a job which the employee can perform (occasionally known as assigning the employee to "light duty"). Even if light duty is assigned, the agency is free to cancel the light duty assignment even years later, and to require the employee to perform in his position of record, or face a disability separation. This is an area that frequently is the subject of collective bargaining, though, so be sure to refer to your union contract and your past practices when dealing with a medically limited employee in a bargaining unit.

Disability law can be a very complicated area, even for the experienced practitioner. If you have any doubt about whether your problem employee has a disability and is entitled to the reasonable accommodation process, be sure to consult with the reasonable accommodation experts within your agency. You don't have to do this alone.

Perhaps most of all, be sure to remember that what we've laid out above are your minimal responsibilities. If you are dealing with a good employee who has a medical condition, but who does not have a disability, you may choose to adapt the workplace so that the employee is able to continue working. In this book, we tend to focus on the problem employee's minimal rights. Don't let this approach prevent you from accommodating the good employee who just needs a little extra help.

Access to medical information and fitness for duty examinations – When dealing with employees who have medical problems, supervisors often want reliable medical information beyond what the employee says about his condition; they often want a report from a physician about the employee's medical condition, prognosis, and specific restrictions. Up until about 30 years ago, all a supervisor had to do in this situation was to send the employee to a "fitness for duty" examination, a medical examination conducted by an agency-selected physician who would send a medical report back to the supervisor for his use in deciding what to do. That all changed in the early '80s when employees complained to Congress that the very act of sending an employee to be examined medically was overly intrusive, adverse, and an invasion of privacy. This was particularly thought to be true when the medical examination included a psychiatric evaluation of the employee, because these results were often seen by people beyond those management officials who had a need to know.

In response, the Office of Personnel Management took away the authority for federal supervisors to routinely send employees to fitness for duty examinations. Instead, a medical examination can be ordered by an agency only when certain criteria are met. Those criteria are laid out in 5 C.F.R. § 339.30. As of this writing, they are as follows:

> Authority to require an examination.
>
> (a) A routine pre-appointment examination is appropriate only for a position which has specific medical standards, physical requirements, or is covered by a medical evaluation program established under these regulations.
> (b) Subject to Sec. 339.103 of this part, an agency may require an individual who has applied for or occupies a position which has medical standards or physical requirements or which is part of an established medical evaluation program, to report for a medical examination:
> (1) Prior to appointment or selection (including reemployment on the basis of full or partial recovery from a medical condition);
> (2) On a regularly recurring, periodic basis after appointment; or
> (3) Whenever there is a direct question about an employee's continued capacity to meet the physical or medical requirements of aposition.
> (c) An agency may require an employee who has applied for or is receiving continuation of pay or compensation as a result of an on-

thejob injury or disease to report for an examination to determine medical limitations that may affect placement decisions.

(d) An agency may require an employee who is released from his or her competitive level in a reduction in force to undergo a relevantmedical evaluation if the position to which the employee has reassignment rights has medical standards or specific physical requirements which are different from those required in the employee's current position.

(e)(1) An agency may order a psychiatric examination (including a psychological assessment) only when:

(i) The result of a current general medical examination which the agency has the authority to order under this section indicates no physical explanation for behavior or actions which may affect the safeand efficient performance of the individual or others, or

(ii) A psychiatric examination is specifically called for in a position having medical standards or subject to a medical evaluation program established under this part.

(2) A psychiatric examination or psychological assessment authorized under (i) or (ii) above must be conducted in accordance with accepted professional standards, by a licensed practitioner or physician authorized to conduct such examinations, and may only be used to make legitimate inquiry into a person's mental fitness to successfully perform the duties of his or her position without undue hazard to the individual or others.

Most federal positions do not have specific medical standards or physical requirements, and few positions are involved in an ongoing medical evaluation program. Medical standards, if established, are usually specified as a separate attachment to an employee's official Position Description. Physical requirements sometimes are specified in the body of the position description, e.g., "Must be able to lift 40 pounds." Absent such specifications, though, the agency usually is without the authority to order an employee to be medically examined.

So, what do you do when the employee claims a medical condition and asks for some benefit or accommodation because of that condition, and you want more detailed reliable medical information before responding to the request?

Simple. Deny the request until the employee brings the medical information you tell him you need. He wants a brighter light to read by because he has macular degeneration? Give him a letter that tells him exactly what information you want from his physician. Usually that would include things like the physician's diagnosis of the employee's problem, his prognosis, and the medical examinations on which he has based his medical judgment. In addition, you may want the physician to review the employee's position description and to state which job duties would be affected by the medical condition, in what way they would be affected, and whether there is any way the physician thinks that the duties could be modified so that they could be performed. If the employee refuses your request for information, you simply refuse the request for the benefit or accommodation the employee is seeking.

Always keep the responsibility for producing the medical information on the employee. Do not place that responsibility on yourself by telling the employee that you will look into the matter and then try to get his physician to release the information to you. Do not ask the employee to sign a medical release and then spend your time trying to get the treating physician to respond to the release with copies of the employee's medical records. THE RESPONSIBILITY IS THE EMPLOYEE'S. If he doesn't produce the documentation you need, you don't have a legal obligation to grant the request.

A nice alternative to include in any discussion about obtaining medical information can steer the employee toward a more reliable source of medical information than the employee's family physician who, if he is unethical, will very likely color his report to support his patient/client. See how this sounds to you:

> *John, I realize that you would like to have your schedule converted to a half-time position because of the recent onset of chronic fatigue syndrome. However, the note you've given me from Dr. Crackpot doesn't provide me enough information on which to make a decision. I can give you a letter to take to Dr. Crackpot that tells him all the tests we need to see and asks him for much more specific information, and you can make an appointment*

> *with him to go over that. However, if you would prefer a simpler option, I can make an appointment for you to be seen by Dr. Goodguy, an agency physician who can see you right away, and the agency will pay for the examination. His report will come directly to me and I can make a decision as soon as I get the information from him. He's very good and very fast, so we should be able to take care of this thing quickly. How does that sound?*

By offering the employee the opportunity to be seen for free by an agency-selected physician, you may be able to reap the advantage of impartiality that the old fitness for duty examination provided without violating OPM regulations by directing an examination. If the employee declines your magnanimous offer, you're stuck with receiving a medical report from a health care provider who may not have the agency's interest as a top priority. However, you are free to continue to decline the request for a benefit or accommodation until Dr. Crackpot provides you with acceptable evidence of the medical limitation.

Recommended tactic – Some employment law practitioners advocate ordering employees to produce medical evidence that they are medically fit to perform their duties. We would suggest that approach is fraught with difficulties and should be avoided if at all possible. The more straightforward way to approach medical problems follows this sequence of logic and action:

1. First, determine whether the employee's medical problem rises to the level of a disability. This determination will require consultation with your agency's experts in disability accommodation. If you find the employee has a disability, go to step 2. If not, go to step 4.
2. If the employee has a disability, he is entitled to a reasonable accommodation of that disability if he is a qualified individual, as discussed above. If an accommodation is obvious, feel free to implement it. If it is not, you are obligated by law to engage in the interactive process with the employee in an attempt to identify an accommodation that will allow the employee to perform acceptably. You still get to choose which option to implement as an accommodation, but you are required to discuss

the options with the employee rather than to conclude that no accommodation is available. You don't have to do this alone; your reasonable accommodation coordinator should also be involved in the interactive process.

3. Once accommodated, the employee should be held to the same standards of performance and conduct as would a non-disabled employee. If the employee has a psychological condition that causes him to be rude and discourteous to agency clients, he can be disciplined for being rude and discourteous as would a non-disabled co-worker. If one of the critical performance standards for his position requires a minimum keyboarding rate of 40 words per minute, he can be fired for unacceptable performance if his rate is below that and the agency has otherwise accommodated his medical limitation (e.g. given him a keyboard that is easier for him to use) and no other accommodation would allow him to meet that standard.
4. If the employee does not meet the legal definition of a qualified person with a disability, you should move forward with discipline or a performance Demonstration Plan, depending on the problem situation you have. Include the following in your approach:
    a. Approve only the leave requests you must and deny all other (usually that means denying requests for LWOP and advanced sick and annual leave; you should even deny requests for participation in the agency's pool of donated leave).
    b. Require the employee to produce acceptable medical evidence; don't try to get the information yourself.
    c. Investigate whether the employee is eligible for disability retirement. If he is, explain to him the benefits of taking a voluntary disability retirement as compared to undergoing an involuntary termination for misconduct or poor performance.
5. As an alternative to a misconduct or poor performance removal, consider terminating the employee based on a charge of "Medical Inability to Perform." If you are able to obtain medical information adequate to establish that the employee cannot perform one

(or more) of the critical elements of his position, then you can separate him for medical inability to perform without having to undergo a DP or to consider progressive discipline. The employee may be able to get disability retirement, discontinued service retirement, or even unemployment benefits from the state after such a separation. Although those are separate matters, as part of the inability-to-perform termination process, you may want to explain these potential benefits to the employee. If these benefits are indeed available, the employee may be much less likely to appeal or grieve the termination. Being fired for medical inability to perform just might be the best thing that ever happened to him.

Every federal supervisor will undoubtedly encounter each one of these situations in his federal career. You have the authority and the tools to succeed in these complicated scenarios – so go out there and do it.

CHAPTER 7
AGGRESSIVE STRATEGIES

In the previous chapters, we have gone into great detail as to how to use the more standard procedures for dealing with problem employees in government. As a reminder and to give you some perspective for this chapter, in general they are:

If the problem is misconduct –

1. Establish a rule and notify the employee.
2. Reprimand for a first violation of the rule.
3. Suspend for a second violation.
4. Terminate for a third violation.

If the problem is unacceptable performance as measured by the employee's performance standards –

1. Issue the performance standards.
2. Allow a period of time to perform.
3. Implement a Demonstration Period.
4. Remove at the end of an unsuccessful DP.

These procedures are the most common approaches that supervisors take with problem employees. However, as anyone who has gone through one of these processes as a supervisor will tell you, dealing with a problem employee using the standard procedures takes time and support resources, and the chances are about one in five that you will lose on appeal.

That is why the more experienced supervisors consider all the options available when confronted with a non-performing or misbehaving employee. In this chapter, we will discuss five creative - even aggressive - ways of dealing with problem employees outside of the standard procedures.

Now, please don't take these options the wrong way. We are not telling you ways to "game" the system or to misuse procedures in an unfair manner against employees simply because you don't like them. If that is what you're looking for, you will have to look elsewhere. What we do below is explain five perfectly legitimate options for reducing or eliminating the harm caused by a problem employee; options that will save you a lot of time and heartache if they happen to fit your particular situation. Although these options are not appropriate in all circumstances, they are viable alternatives in more situations than many supervisors realize.

So here we go.

Option One: Directed Geographic Reassignment – Move the Problem

Many employees do not realize that even though they were hired into government in a particular work location and have worked there many years, they have no entitlement to continue to work in that location. The employing agency can transfer an employee to any location at which it has a need for the employee's services. As long as the agency is willing to pay for the expenses related to a move, an employee can be reassigned to a permanent position at the same grade on relatively short notice (maybe 60 days or less) and the employee's choice is either to accept the move and begin work in the new location or resign. If the employee refuses either option, the agency can separate him for refusing to accept a work location reassignment.

If the employee is terminated for refusing to accept the order to relocate, on appeal the burden of proof will be on the employee to show that the reassignment was motivated by improper reasons; e.g., that the supervisor who ordered the reassignment did not do it for job-related reasons, but rather did it because of the employee's race, sex, color, national origin, religion, disability, age, genetic profile, status as a veteran, activity on behalf of a union, or in reprisal for the employee's whistleblowing, participation in the discrimination complaint process, or prior grievance/appeal activity. This listing, by the way, is a listing of "protected categories" within the federal government. When you hear someone speak of membership in a protected category, they are almost always referring to one of these groups.

The agency's burden is to prove that the reassignment was for bona fide (i.e. legitimate) management reasons. It does not have to prove that the reassignment was absolutely necessary or the only available option; it simply must establish that the employee's services would be of value to the agency elsewhere.

This is often a straightforward matter to establish with a problem employee. For example, consider the situation in which the employee, a budget analyst, just isn't getting the job done. He is right at the line between minimally acceptable and unacceptable performance, does not get along with his supervisor, and has trouble with his coworkers (who probably have to do some of his work in addition to their own). The supervisor could put the employee on a DP or start progressive discipline. However, if the agency could use the services of a budget analyst in another work location, it could give the employee a directed reassignment and order the employee relocated to that work site. When challenged on appeal, the agency could honestly say that the reason for the transfer was to try to find an environment in which the employee might have a chance to perform at a higher level, to give him a chance to succeed as he was at or near failure in his current location.

As a result of the directed reassignment order, one of two things will happen:

1. The employee will refuse the reassignment and either resign or be terminated. If this happens, the problem is solved without having to endure progressive discipline or an unacceptable performance action. Or,

2. The employee will accept the reassignment. If this happens, the employee will either be successful in the new work location, or fail. If successful, then you have avoided entirely the need to take discipline or a performance action. If his performance is unacceptable, you are no worse off than you were to begin with (except for the expense of the move).

Oh, we can hear the moans from some readers at this very moment: "I can't do something like this! It's just passing on problems from one supervisor to the next." Or, "Look at the cost of the move. I could never justify an expense like that." Well, stop moaning. The reality is that some employees, some relatively bad employees, actually perform acceptably when reassigned to a different supervisor and/or a different environment. You are doing something pro-employee when you are flexible enough to offer the individual an opportunity to work in a different location. As for the expense of the move, if you think a $20,000 moving bill is a lot of money, compare it to the employee's annual expense to the agency for a pay check plus benefits he's been taking home for years and to the $100,000 litigation costs to the government if you were to use one of the standard methods of removing the employee.

There are three lesser aspects of directed reassignments that may be helpful to you should you choose to go this way, so keep them in mind:

1. Employees who refuse directed reassignments and are terminated are eligible for state unemployment benefits (employees who are fired for misconduct usually are not so entitled). For some employees, knowledge of this benefit just might make a separation a palatable alternative to fighting an adverse action removal.
2. Federal employees who refuse directed reassignments can start to receive an immediate annuity if they meet the age and time in service requirements for a discontinued service retirement. For many, this is a very acceptable alternative to an adverse action termination. This may well be a valuable bit of information if you find yourself bargaining with the employee or his representative.

3. For non-SES employees, agencies must prove that there is a bona fide reason for the reassignment. However, for SES employees, the agency can get by with less – it must prove only that the employee is qualified for reassignment.

If you would like to read more about directed reassignments, go to MSPB's web site, www.mspb.gov, and look for *Shenwick v. State*, 92 M.S.P.R. 289 (2002), a nicely crafted decision that will point you toward lots of authority for you to do what we've talked about in this section.

Consider a directed reassignment as an investment, an investment that hopefully will pay off, for both the employee and the agency. But even if it does not, the risk is usually worth the potential gain.

Option Two: Reduced Work Schedule – Reduce the Harm

Joe hasn't done a lick of work in years; he's just sort of passing time until retirement or his lottery number comes up, whichever is first. Not a misconduct problem, more of a no-conduct problem. He doesn't really hurt you that much, but he doesn't do anything for you, either. If he didn't come to work for a few weeks, you probably wouldn't even notice very much, except that everyone else would be in a better mood without him around.

You've thought about initiating an unacceptable performance action, but you already have too much on your plate and you know those things take time. Besides, you might lose on appeal (the chances are one in five) and then all that work would be for nothing. So, what's a supervisor going to do?

Well, if Joe isn't doing you any good while pulling down a $60,000 a year salary, how about cutting him to part-time and saving a big chunk of that yearly expense? If he doesn't get anything done in a 40-hour week, why not let him get nothing done in eight hours of pay instead? With the money you save in his salary, you should be able to hire another part-timer who really wants to work and who can run circles around Joe. Perhaps you could even help an individual with a disability that limits her work hours to find employment, or make it easier for a parent who wants to spend more time with the kids. Yes, reducing Joe to part-time and recruiting another part-timer to do the work that Joe should have been doing will be a win-win situation.

But can't Joe file a complaint or grievance about the reduced work hours? Sure, he can; an employee can file a grievance or complaint about just about anything. Will he win? Surprisingly, no he won't (unless you are as foolish as to reduce his schedule because of his membership in one of those "protected categories" we talked about in the previous section). All you will have to do is to articulate a valid reason for the reduction, and Joe's low performance is just about as valid a reason as you can get. Government employees are not entitled to full time work for their entire careers, and as the supervisor you have the option of reducing the work schedule to fit your needs.

Those of you who have been paying attention throughout the previous pages might remember that the Merit Systems Protection Board has jurisdiction over reductions in pay or demotions. Certainly, someone who has been reduced from working 40 hours per week to only 8 or so has suffered a "reduction in pay," correct? Interestingly, the Board, with support from the federal courts, has held that it does NOT have jurisdiction over a reduced number of work hours even though the result is what a layman would consider to be a reduction in pay. If you're a stickler for authority, you can find that by reading a couple of sample decisions available in most any law library or on the web, *Wolf v. VA*, 87 MSPR 33 (2000) and *Axtman v. Interior*, 926 F.2d 1120 (1991).

The bottom line is that simply reducing the offending employee's work schedule to some level less than full employment is a lot easier than taking a standard misconduct or performance action, should reduce the drain on the organization from having the guy around all the time, and just might encourage him to go work elsewhere. Hiring a part-time replacement to actually do the work would be the icing on this little cake of an option to the traditional procedures.

Option Three: Last Chance Agreement – Cut a Deal

Let's say that you have gone to the trouble to use progressive discipline to deal with a conduct problem, and you are at the stage where removal would be reasonable for the most recent offense using the standard procedures. However, you know there is no guarantee if you terminate the employee that he will not somehow get his job back on appeal.

If the harm the employee has caused has not been too terribly bad, you may be interested in considering an option that will give the employee one more opportunity to demonstrate acceptable conduct while simultaneously allowing you to avoid having to defend your actions should a subsequent removal become necessary. Here's how it works:

1. The employee has engaged in two or three acts of misconduct. He has been previously suspended and you are ready to begin the termination process (you may also get to this point if the employee's only act of misconduct is so harmful to you that under the Douglas Factors, removal would be a defensible penalty selection).
2. Tell the employee that you are intending to propose his removal. Alternatively, you may want to go ahead and propose the removal, and then discuss this option with the employee after the response period has passed, but before the decision letter has been issued. Your choice here depends on your relationship with the employee. Either way you go is OK. The main point is that it is essential that the employee knows his job is on the line and that you are ready to terminate him for his most recent infraction.
3. Explain to the employee that you are prepared to go forward with the removal action, but that you are also willing to consider an alternative: You will be willing to hold the tentative removal in abeyance for one year (or six months or two years or whatever period of time you want) to give the employee one last opportunity to demonstrate acceptable conduct. If he abstains from any further instances of misconduct during this time, at the end of the abeyance period you will cancel the tentative removal. However,

> in exchange for this opportunity, the employee has to agree that if he engages in any further misconduct during the abeyance period, he will accept a removal without filing an appeal, grievance, or complaint. In other words, he is agreeing to waive his appeal rights in exchange for a last chance to prove himself.

If the employee agrees to this "Last Chance" offer, you should have someone who is an expert in this area of law draft an agreement for both of you to sign. It's not hard to draft a good agreement if you know the case law, but it can be dangerous to draft one if you do not.

If the employee satisfies the year of good behavior requirement, you will have retained a valued government employee. If the employee fails to maintain acceptable conduct, you have an appeal-proof way of terminating his employment. Either way, you come out ahead as compared to the traditional approach of an immediate adverse action termination with full appeal rights. The employee may be able to challenge whether he breached the agreement, but not the merits of the underlying action. And you don't even have to notify him of any appeal rights if subsequently you fire him for breaching the agreement.

Of course, if the employee declines your gracious offer, you are still free to implement the proposed removal action. You've really lost very little by making the Last Chance offer along the way, and will probably make yourself look compassionate and right-minded when you have to defend your action on appeal.

Option Four: Last Rites – Let Him Leave with Dignity

The Last Chance option discussed above is appropriate when dealing with an employee who you believe just might be able to be a productive member of your workforce. The Last Rites option is suitable when you are convinced that the employee has no future with your organization, and he just has to go. Here's how it works:

1. The employee has committed an act of misconduct or poor performance that warrants removal (the Last Chance option is most applicable only in a case of misconduct, in comparison).
2. Prior to proposing a removal, you meet with the employee to tell him it's all over. It is essential that you are absolutely accurate and truthful when you tell the employee at this stage that you have the evidence necessary to propose his removal and that you intend to do so unless the two of you can reach an agreement through these discussions. If you tell the employee that you have the evidence, and it is later proven that you did not, this option will be set aside as a coerced agreement.
3. Then, you tell the employee that you don't necessarily want to record a termination for misconduct in his permanent record and that you are willing to give him some time to find himself another position, but you will only do so in exchange for his promise to resign if his job hunt is unsuccessful.

Perhaps the discussion will go something like this:

> *Joe, you have done a respectable job for the agency for a number of years. However, you have to admit that your performance has deteriorated recently - deteriorated so far in fact that I am going to have to initiate a formal action to have you removed from your position.*
>
> *However, rather than go through the legal process that will result in a termination being recorded on your official record, I'm willing to give you a chance to use your own initiative to find yourself another position that is more in line with your talents. I'm willing to give you the next 60 days to find other employment in exchange for your promise to resign voluntarily at the end of that period even if you have not yet found another job. During those 60 days, you don't have to come to work. I will carry you in a work-at-home status. You can use me as a reference if you like in your job search. If I'm contacted, I'll truthfully tell whoever is calling that you are currently employed with us and that your most recent performance rating was satisfactory. I*

will decline to discuss anything related to the problems you've been happening.

If you decide that you do not want to accept this option, I'll have to go forward with the removal, and you will be able to challenge the final decision through an appeal or grievance. If you resign after a removal is officially proposed, you will need to report that to any other government agency should you seek future employment.

Take a couple of days to think it over and discuss this with an attorney, your union representative, or anyone else whose opinion you trust. I'll be happy to talk with anyone you would like me to about what I'm proposing. However, I need your answer by the close of business on Friday. If I don't hear from you by then, I'll have to initiate the removal the first of next week.

If the employee accepts your magnanimous offer, ask one of your expert management support staff members to draft a Last Rites agreement for you both to sign. That way, the employee can't get to day 59 and then decide he'd like to withdraw his agreement and ride out a formal removal. By that time, you will have an enforceable contract because you have given the employee something of value (60 days without assigned duties) in exchange for his promise to resign. Lawyers just love this exchange of consideration stuff and any arbitrator, board, or court in the country will enforce the provisions as long as everybody's honest about their motives and fulfills each aspect of their responsibilities under the agreement.

Uh-oh. We're starting to hear moaning again: "Sixty days of paid absence! Do I look like I'm running a charity here! I'm not going to give a vacation to a loser like Joe, let alone a neutral job reference."

Hey, Joe hasn't done a decent day's work in years. He's been pulling home a big government salary for not doing anything for a long time; another two months isn't going to kill you. Besides, compared to the $100,000 that the Government Accountability Office says a formal removal action costs the federal government, 60 days of pay is peanuts (OK, big peanuts, but still a small legume in comparison).

And, look what you've bought for your money:

- Immediate removal of Joe from the workplace. No 30-day notice, no 30-day DP. One day he's here, the next day he's not. Now THAT ought to get the attention of some of his coworkers who also may be drifting toward the dark side and a termination action themselves.
- Guaranteed outcome of Joe being gone forever without the chance of being reversed on appeal.
- Little staff time and even less animosity to make all this happen as compared to gearing up for a standard removal action.
- And perhaps more important than anything else (come on, we don't have to be the tough guy all the time), you may have allowed Joe the opportunity to keep his head up with his family and friends, and to get on with his life in a respectable manner. Remember, just because he was not a good employee for you does not necessarily mean that he might not be acceptable in another situation.

So, have a big heart and at the same time, buy yourself a sweet deal by offering a Last Rites agreement to employees who might find one to be acceptable, and who deserve to get on with their life.

A variation on this approach that works in some organizations is known as a "Terminal Detail." The discussion and the objectives are the same as in the classic Last Rites approach. However, instead of offering the employee paid time to find another job, the supervisor offers the employee a chance to go work for some other supervisor in the hope that will give him time to either be hired permanently by that supervisor or find another position somewhere else:

1. Have a meeting with the employee to explain that removal is imminent if he stays in his current position, as done in the Last Rites approach.
2. Then, tell the employee that you will give him two weeks to find another supervisor in the organization who is willing to have the employee work for him. Tell the employee that he can inform the

other supervisor that you will retain the employee on your payroll while he is performing work for the new supervisor.

3. The receiving supervisor benefits from getting work from the employee without the pay coming out of his budget. It also gives the receiving supervisor a chance to observe the employee closely, in case he decides he has a permanent position in which the employee can perform.
4. The operative document is a detail by the current supervisor to the new supervisor for some specific period of time; three to six months is typical, but the trial period is fully negotiable.
5. Have the employee sign an agreement that says he understands that the detail is temporary, and that he agrees to resign at the end of the detail if he has not found alternative employment by then.

The Terminal Detail option has the benefit of avoiding the paid-time-off-with-pay approach of the classic Last Rites alternative. In addition, it puts the onus on the employee to find alternative employment rather than on the supervisor. Unfortunately, it does not make sense in all organizations and thereby lacks the universal attraction of a Last Rites agreement.

Keep in mind that if the employee occupies a position in a collective bargaining unit (union), the union has a right to assign a representative to be in meetings in which you discuss options like the Last Rites. Such meetings are known by law as "formal discussions." Be sure to coordinate with your labor relations advisor prior to meeting with the employee to attempt to negotiate an alternative to removal.

Option Five: Revoke His Security Clearance – Protect Our Country

If the employee who is causing a problem has an agency-issued security clearance, the U.S. Supreme Court has held that the granting and revocation of that security clearance is so fundamentally attached to the Constitutional responsibilities of the President that security clearance matters are unreviewable outside of the agency's internal procedures. In other words, an agency can revoke an employee's security clearance using whatever notice and response procedures it cares to develop, terminate the employee for failing to maintain a security clearance, and it will never have to defend its revocation to anyone - not in an appeal to the Merit System Protection Board, in a discrimination complaint to the Equal Employment Opportunity Commission, before an arbitrator, before the Federal Labor Relations Authority, or to the Office of Special Counsel. That's how important Congress and the courts believe the security of our country is to us all.

Even if the employee has irrefragable proof that the agency revoked his security clearance because of his national origin and that he blew the whistle on government waste while serving as a union official and that the agency's "charges" against him are completely falsified, he has no direct access to court to protect himself. He might be able to rely on public pressure or Congressional assistance, but that's about it. Like it or not, the ability to revoke an employee's security clearance and to then fire him for failing to maintain a clearance is the Big Hammer in the supervisor's tool box when confronted with a misbehaving employee. The only limits or time constraints are those imposed by the agency itself, and it is free to modify those constraints without intervention from outside sources whenever it wants.

The bottom line is that if your problem employee occupies a position that the agency has identified as requiring a security clearance, and if the employee engages in conduct incompatible with retaining that clearance, the revocation of the clearance may be the best way to terminate the employee from employment without having to defend that action to an outside third party. If your agency's clearance revocation procedures are too cumbersome and attenuated, you may want to lobby hard at your next management retreat for some streamlining and simplification. The ability to independently revoke security clearances is a HUGELY powerful tool in the right circumstances.

There are two caveats should you choose to go this way:

1. An employee who is terminated for losing a security clearance is considered to have been terminated for non-disciplinary reasons. Therefore, he is eligible for unemployment benefits and even a

discontinued service early retirement if he meets the length of service criteria.

2. Keep in mind that a security clearance can be revoked for behaviors that cannot be characterized as misconduct. For example, a government employee who chooses to marry an individual who has relatives in another country and who could be subjected to blackmail or untoward pressure by a foreign government because of those familial relations could lose his security clearance even though there is no misconduct involved in marrying someone with overseas relatives.

Option Six: Termination in Eight Days - Take Him Out. Now.

The image that the general public has of misbehaving government employees and ineffective government supervisors almost qualifies as a horror picture, doesn't it?

- The employee is rude, crude, and engages in vile disgusting conduct every chance he has, and gets no work done.
- The poor supervisor, even when his intentions are good, is held back and slowed down by an overly-burdensome system of employee rights, responses, appeals, and other delays that prevent the termination of the employee even when every citizen in America knows that the guy should go.
- The government grinds to a halt, even the good employees give up the fight, and the (flu bugs, terrorists, undocumented aliens – pick your scariest option) invade our shores, lay waste to our cities, and cause the end of Our Way of Life.

There's even a belief that the Fall of Rome was actually caused by a single bad civil servant who just could not be fired and who refused to retire even when eligible because he was having so much fun mucking things up. Yes, when it comes to the popular misconception of disciplining government employees, the destined-for-Oscar film based on this image might be labeled a documentary rather than fiction. Wouldn't it be great for our government, nay – our entire civilization – if a federal employee could be fired in just over a week after the act of misconduct occurred and still have all the rights and privileges of due process provided to him in a legal manner? Well, we are here at this moment to tell you that a speedy termination can indeed be invoked legally, and that a misbehaving federal civil servant can be excised from the workforce in less time than most supervisors ever imagined. This procedure can't be implemented in every instance of misconduct, but when it can – when the shoe fits – a fast termination can do wonders to cleanse a workplace of a disruptive debilitating force, while simultaneously sending a message to the remaining employees that if you screw up, you'll be out of a job before next week's church bulletin is delivered. Here's how it works:

A federal employee is entitled by law to a minimum of 30-days' notice prior to a termination. In practice, this means that after the supervisor has collected enough evidence to determine that removal is warranted, the supervisor can issue the employee a letter proposing termination, the employee may respond to the letter, and the deciding official can issue a decision to remove effective no sooner than 30 days from the date of the proposal letter. The first day of the 30-day period is the day after the day on which the proposal is issued, so from start to finish, a minimum of 31 days is required by law.

With one exception.

There is a provision in law known as the "crime provision." That provision says that the minimum 30-day advanced written notice period prior to a termination does NOT apply when the supervisor has:

> *Reasonable cause to believe the employee has committed a crime for which imprisonment may be imposed. 5 U.S.C. § 7513(a)(1).*

Read alone, one could fairly draw the conclusion that no notice period at all is required whenever there is proof that the employee has committed a jail-worthy crime. However, the very next section of law (5 U.S.C. § 7513(a) (2)) says that in all cases, an employee is entitled to at least seven days to respond to the notice of proposed removal. Read together, as laws must be, an employee whose act of misconduct was to have committed a crime from which imprisonment might result is entitled to a minimum of eight days of notice before he can be terminated. It could be this simple:

1. This morning happens to be a Monday. The supervisor acquires enough evidence (i.e., a "reasonable cause to believe") that the employee committed a crime punishable by imprisonment.
2. This afternoon, the supervisor specifically references the crime provision (very important) in his proposal letter, and proposes that the employee be terminated from government service.
3. Tomorrow, Tuesday, is the initial day of the mandatory seven-day minimum opportunity to respond period. During the response period, the deciding official accepts and considers any oral or written response the employee cares to make.
4. Next Monday is the seventh and last day of the response period. As it is unclear from the law whether the employee has to be given until midnight of that day to respond or only until the normal close of business for his shift, to be safe the deciding official does not issue the final decision letter until Tuesday, making the termination effective at the beginning of the shift.

From the day the supervisor obtains proof of the crime (Monday) until the day the employee is off the rolls (the following Tuesday as early as the beginning of the shift) just over a week has transpired. For the purpose of having a number we can refer to, let's say that's a total of eight days from misconduct to termination.

Not bad for government work.

Now, why have you not heard of this rocket-docket procedure before? Or, if you have, why is it not more widely used? Well, there are several factors involved in what should otherwise be a straightforward application of the crime provision law – factors that have developed as cases have been adjudicated by the Board and the courts. In no particular order, here are concerns you will have if you attempt to implement this procedure:

Applying complex, sparse, inconsistent case law

The 22 words that make up the crime provision are not complicated on first read. The complication comes from the decisions that are issued by the courts and the Board after the law went into effect. Reducing a notice period from 30 days to only 7 is a big deal in the eyes of many adjudicators. The tendency of the judges who review these cases is to want to find highly exceptional circumstances that would warrant such a rights reduction.

Unfortunately, the law itself does not define any highly exceptional circumstances other than that the agency must reasonably believe the employee committed a crime that could result in imprisonment. The agency does not have to prove the crime was actually committed, only that its belief is reasonable. That's an awfully low evidentiary standard. In addition, the employee does not need to have committed a particularly egregious crime according to the law, only a crime for which imprisonment might result, even if the possible imprisonment is for a very brief time. There are lots of crimes in our society that by law provide for possible imprisonment, even though imprisonment is rarely ordered and even though the maximum period of incarceration is measured in days rather than months or years. However slight the crime, if the statute that establishes the crime says that imprisonment is possible, then the crime provision can be applied.

A big part of the problem is that the judiciary and the quasi-judiciary are left with a situation in which the law seems out of line with reality; that a major right of a government employee can be reduced by an act of misconduct that just isn't that big a deal. The result is that adjudicators who have reviewed cases involving the crime provision had wrestled mightily to make the legal glove fit the factual situation and they have met with mixed success. Sometimes the adjudicators get it right, and sometimes they do not.

In addition, because the law is so unsettled and because there are other tried-and-true (though less expedient) options, many agencies decide not to invoke the crime provision. Therefore, few cases get adjudicated and little is added to the body of case law by which we interpret the statute; the law has therefore remained obtuse and unresolved, adding to an agency's hesitance to invoke the provision. The cycle feeds on itself.

Defining "reasonable cause" to believe a crime has been committed

Legislators intentionally use terms such as "reasonable cause" when drafting legislation aware that such terms are inexact phrases subject to judicial interpretation. In some ways that is a good because it allows the law to grow and develop over time and allows judges and other adjudicators flexibility in dealing with specific situations. In other ways, such inexact wording simply causes uncertainty and confusion because the individual who has to decide how to act has to do so without complete guidance until after the case is adjudicated. Inexactness can result in agencies not knowing what to do, and thereby causing the agency not to act at all. Consider the following fact set taken from a real case (*Davis v. TVA,* 11 MSPR 367 (1982)):

1. An agency check for $250 was missing.
2. A store owner notified the agency that he had cashed the check.
3. The store owner was familiar with the check casher.
4. The store owner wrote down the license plate number of the check casher.
5. The police traced the license plate to the agency's employee.
6. The employee was arrested.
7. The employee was incarcerated temporarily.
8. The employee was indicted, and a trial date was set.

The Board considered all of these facts and determined that the agency had "reasonable cause" to conclude that the employee had committed the crime of "uttering and passing a forged instrument" and that invoking the crime provision was proper.

But how does this help us in a similar situation that occurs later when the facts are close, but a little different? What if facts 1 through 7 existed, but not number 8? Is that enough to meet the "reasonable cause" standard? Or, what if fact number 7 is missing? Is there "reasonable cause?" An inherent problem in this field of law, as in many fields of law, is that we really don't know what will pass legal muster until we take the chance, do it, and then see how a judge adjudicates the matter. This uncertainty is one of the reasons that agencies use more familiar alternatives rather than taking a chance in an untested area.

Separating direct knowledge situations from secondary knowledge situations

There are two distinct ways in which an agency comes to know that an employee has engaged in criminal misconduct:

- *Direct knowledge* – The employee sneaks into the office one weekend using a stolen key and takes a laptop computer. On Monday, the agency's security officer shows the surveillance videotape of the taking to the supervisor to the employee's supervisor and informs the supervisor that the employee later sold the laptop to an undercover police officer. The supervisor knows that the employee was not authorized to take and sell the agency's laptop and the agency's legal counsel informs the supervisor that the employee's conduct meets the statutory definition of theft of government property. The supervisor now has direct knowledge of facts which would support a probable cause belief the employee committed a crime for which imprisonment may result.

- *Secondary knowledge* – The supervisor has no personal knowledge of any misconduct. However, he becomes aware through a newspaper article or through reports from contacts from local law enforcement that the employee has been arrested on the suspicion that he has stolen government property, and that there has been some sort of preliminary judicial action. There may or may not be enough evidence to establish a probable cause to believe a crime has been committed, depending on several factors that may be present in the case.

The second situation above, the secondary knowledge situation, has caused the most litigation. You are invited to read the many convoluted court decisions that have wrestled with this issue, but the bottom line today is this: The crime provision CANNOT be invoked based solely on the fact that an employee has been arrested or even that there was an arrest and an arraignment. However, if the arrest is accompanied by a judicially issued criminal complaint or indictment, then the agency CAN invoke the crime provision even though it has no direct evidence of the misconduct itself.

The secondary knowledge situation is not quite so clear cut. Without some sort of minimal judicial determination, the agency must look to the other facts it has and take its best guess if the information before it will be sufficient to justify use of the crime provision. We know that an arrest alone is not enough. However, an arrest coupled with the agency's independent investigation of the same incident causing the arrest may well satisfy the reasonable cause burden. Unfortunately, the few cases we have to rely on cover just a few of the situations that can arise, so an agency acts without firm guidance when trying to establish that a collection of evidence is enough to invoke the crime provision.

Defending the penalty selection

The invocation of the crime provision is most frequently paired with the penalty of an indefinite suspension. Indefinite suspensions are favored by agencies in these situations for two reasons:

- An indefinite suspension for the purpose of investigating further the facts surrounding a particular situation can be defended based on the REASONABLE BELIEF that misconduct has occurred, and does not require the agency to prove at this stage of the game that the alleged misconduct was ACTUALLY COMMITTED. The theory is that the indefinite suspension will allow the agency time to conduct a more extensive investigation and propose an appropriate disciplinary action (probably termination) based on the results of the investigation.

- An indefinite suspension of an employee during a period of time the employee is defending himself in a criminal proceeding protects the employee's rights in the criminal forum (e.g., the right against self-incrimination and the right

> to not have to disclose his defense to the criminal charges by defending himself on the merits of the allegations in an administrative forum such as MSPB). The employee, of course, has a right to appeal the indefinite suspension.

However, just because an indefinite suspension is a common pairing with the implementation of the crime provision does not mean that an indefinite suspension is the only possible discipline that can be administered. The law allows for the crime provision to be used in cases of suspensions, demotions, and terminations so long as the probable cause conditions are met. Therefore, if the agency has proof at the preponderance of the evidence level that the employee committed an act of misconduct that constitutes both a crime for which imprisonment may be imposed AND satisfies a Douglas Factor analysis that would support a termination, the agency can invoke the shortened notice period for the purpose of terminating the employee for the underlying misconduct.

Whatever you do, do NOT make the mistake of believing that an employee can automatically be fired just because you can prove he committed a crime. There still has to be a nexus between the misconduct and the employee's government duties and a supporting Douglas Factor analysis. Make this mistake and you will have the employee back walking your halls before his criminal case ever gets to a jury.

In addition, the Federal Circuit Court of Appeals has stated that the crime believed to be committed must be "serious" and "significantly related" to the work the employee performs. See *Dunnington v. DoJ*, 956 F.2d 1151 (Fed. Cir. 1992). It's a bit unclear whether this admonition applies to invocation of the crime provision alone or invocation of the crime provision coupled with an indefinite suspension. However, the careful practitioner will be aware of the court's unfortunate overstatement of the requirements of the law and take extra steps to establish that the crime is not trivial and is directly related to the employee's assigned work.

Assessing the real value of the crime provision

Some practitioners would argue that with all these problems and unknowns relative to invoking the crime provision, an agency simply is better off to avoid it altogether and to use the more traditional 30-day notice period for dealing with an employee who engage in crimes. There is much to be said for this position.

Yes, if an employee engages in criminal misconduct for which imprisonment may be imposed, the crime provision shortened notice period can be implemented. However, the standard 30-day notice period also can be invoked without the risks involved in using a poorly tested piece of obscure legislation. The only advantage of using the crime provision is to get the employee off of the government payroll just as soon as possible. It is up to you as the supervisor to decide if this additional efficiency is worth the effort.

An astute supervisor can get the employee out of the government workplace immediately upon becoming aware of the misconduct, regardless of whether the crime provision is going to be invoked. All he has to do is to direct the employee to leave the worksite (sometimes accompanied by friendly Officer O'Reilly of the Federal Protective Service) and not return until ordered to do so. So long as the supervisor carries the employee in a pay status (probably investigative leave) and the employee gets paid even though he is performing no duties, the problem has been removed from the workplace without resorting to an appealable suspension or other "challengeable" personnel action. The supervisor can then indulge in the longer 30-day notice period without having to have the employee on-site, and most coworkers may conclude that the employee has already been fired.

By the way, we are familiar with a case many years ago in which a supervisor at a large unnamed government agency (the one with the sailors and the ships) directed an obstreperous employee to, "Get out of here and don't come back until we call you!" As the employee was dutifully placed on paid leave by the timekeeper and sent home without duties, there was no appealable disciplinary action, even though the paid leave lasted over a year and the agency never set about to implement a disciplinary action against the employee! In fact, the employee might still today be drawing a nice little government paycheck for not working if he had not foolishly written to the President of the United States stating that he thought the agency's action was a waste of taxpayer dollars. Some might say he deserved a cash award for blowing the whistle on the agency's wasteful actions. Unfortunately for him, however, the outcome was that the agency realized it had forgotten to fire him, and then did. As we frequently hear when it comes to a government workplace, no good deed goes unpunished.

We give you the crime provision as an optional tool, one that you may choose to avoid because of the potential pitfalls and the precision required to make it work. As tricky as it might be to do it right, we still recommend it to you in the right situation even though there is another option available to you that might do the job almost as well. Given the widely-held misbelief that a government employee simply cannot be fired, doing so in just over a week makes a strong statement for our system of government and just might earn you a special place in the hearts and minds of your colleagues.

If nothing else, you'll make your mom very proud.

If you choose to go this route, you should know …

Crimes for which imprisonment may be imposed: You may be thinking that most of the misconduct that causes you problems are low level misconduct problems, not crimes for which imprisonment may be imposed, and that thereby, the crime provision is of little value to you. The reality is that much misconduct in which a government employee engages fits into the definition of a crime, in part because the employer is a government agency and laws are passed to protect government agencies.

For example, it might be hard to characterize a falsified time card or travel claim filed by a private sector employee as a crime. Although a really creative local prosecutor or district attorney might be able to squeeze the misconduct into the definition of "theft" or "fraudulent divestment of funds through trickery," it would be a tight squeeze. However, a government employee who falsifies a reimbursement or payment claim document has violated federal law, 18 U.S.C. 287, and can be sentenced up to five years in jail:

> Whoever makes or presents to any person or officer in the civil, military, or naval service of the United States, or to any department or agency thereof, any claim upon or against the United States, or any department or agency thereof, knowing such claim to be false, fictitious, or fraudulent, shall be imprisoned not more than five years and shall be subject to a fine in the amount provided in this title.

Although the words of the law make you think of big-ticket crimes, the language of several federal criminal statutes can be easily adapted to apply to misconduct in a federal workplace. Of course, few if any of these acts would actually be prosecuted by an over-worked under-staffed U.S. Attorney's Office because the local U.S. Attorney has a lot of more important things on his plate than routine civil servant misconduct. However, a failure to prosecute makes these incidents no less of a crime under law.

Here are a few examples of what we mean. Our goal here is not to give you a definitive list of federal crimes relative to the workplace, but rather to get you to start thinking about misconduct in these terms, and to consider whether this approach might well be worth pursuing, either on a case-by-case basis or as a policy matter. First, we will give you the wordy legalistic complicated statute itself for you to consider and then give you an example of federal workplace misconduct that would probably meet the definition of the crime and thereby be eligible for invocation of the crime provision should the agency decide to use a shortened notice period:

18 U.S.C. § 4: Whoever, having knowledge of the actual commission of a felony cognizable by a court of the United States, conceals and does not as soon as possible make known the same to some judge or other person in civil or military authority under the United States, shall be fined under this title or imprisoned not more than three years, or both.

Example: An employee knows that a coworker steals supplies from the supply cabinet, covers for the coworker as he sneaks out to his car to hide the supplies, and fails to report the theft to authorities.

18 U.S.C. § 111: (a) In General, whoever—

(1) forcibly assaults, resists, opposes, impedes, intimidates, or interferes with any person designated in section 1114 of this title while engaged in or on account of the performance of official duties; or

(2) forcibly assaults or intimidates any person who formerly served as a person designated in section 1114 on account of the performance of official duties during such person's term of service, shall, where the acts in violation of this section constitute only simple assault, be fined under this title or imprisoned not more than one year, or both, and in all other cases, be fined under this title or imprisoned not more than 8 years, or both.

Example: An employee says to his supervisor, "If you don't give me an Outstanding performance rating this year, I'm going to trash your car."

18 U.S.C. § 115: (1) Whoever—

(A) assaults, kidnaps, or murders, or attempts or conspires to kidnap or murder, or threatens to assault, kidnap or murder a member of the immediate family of a United States official, a United States judge, a Federal law enforcement officer, or an official whose killing would be a crime under section 1114 of this title; or

(B) threatens to assault, kidnap, or murder, a United States official, a United States judge, a Federal law enforcement officer, or an official whose killing would be a crime under such section,

Example: An employee says to his supervisor, "You'd better watch yourself when you talk to me. I know where your children go to school and I know how to use a gun."

18 U.S.C. § 201: (b) Whoever--

(2) being a public official or person selected to be a public official, directly or indirectly, corruptly demands, seeks, receives, accepts, or agrees to receive or accept anything of value personally or for any other person or entity, in return for:

(A) being influenced in the performance of any official act;

(B) being influenced to commit or aid in committing, or to collude in, or allow, any fraud, or make opportunity for the commission of any fraud on the United States; or

(C) being induced to do or omit to do any act in violation of the official duty of such official or person;

shall be fined under this title or not more than three times the monetary equivalent of the thing of value, whichever is greater, or imprisoned for not more than fifteen years, or both, and may be disqualified from holding any office of honor, trust, or profit under the United States.

> *Example: A pharmacist for a health care agency solicits free samples from drug sales representatives for the pharmacist's personal use.*

18 U.S.C. § 208: (a) Except as permitted by subsection (b) hereof, whoever, being an officer or employee of the executive branch of the United States Government, or of any independent agency of the United States, a Federal Reserve bank director, officer, or employee, or an officer or employee of the District of Columbia, including a special Government employee, participates personally and substantially as a Government officer or employee, through decision, approval, disapproval, recommendation, the rendering of advice, investigation, or otherwise, in a judicial or other proceeding, application, request for a ruling or other determination, contract, claim, controversy, charge, accusation, arrest, or other particular matter in which, to his knowledge, he, his spouse, minor child, general partner, organization in which he is serving as officer, director, trustee, general partner or employee, or any person or organization with whom he is negotiating or has any arrangement concerning prospective employment, has a financial interest—

Shall be subject to the penalties set forth in section 216 of this title.

Example: An employee advises a contractor who is bidding on a contract as to what rate of pay has been authorized in other similar contract bids.

18 U.S.C. § 241: If two or more persons conspire to injure, oppress, threaten, or intimidate any person in any State, Territory, Commonwealth, Possession, or District in the free exercise or enjoyment of any right or privilege secured to him by the Constitution or laws of the United States, or because of his having so exercised the same;

They shall be fined under this title or imprisoned not more than ten years, or both.

Example: Two employees develop a scheme to intimidate a coworker into not applying for a specific vacancy.

18 U.S.C. § 242: Whoever, under color of any law, statute, ordinance, regulation, or custom, willfully subjects any person in any State, Territory, Commonwealth, Possession, or District to the deprivation of any rights, privileges, or immunities secured or protected by the Constitution or laws of the United States, or to different punishments, pains, or penalties, on account of such person being an alien, or by reason of his color, or race, than are prescribed for the punishment of citizens, shall be fined under this title or imprisoned not more than one year, or both; and if bodily injury results from the acts committed in violation of this section or if such acts include the use, attempted use, or threatened use of a dangerous weapon, explosives, or fire, shall be fined under this title or imprisoned not more than ten years, or both; and if death results from the acts committed in violation of this section or if such acts include kidnapping or an attempt to kidnap, aggravated sexual abuse, or an attempt to commit aggravated sexual abuse, or an attempt to kill, shall be fined under this title, or imprisoned for any term of years or for life, or both, or may be sentenced to death.

Example: A supervisor refuses to hire an applicant for a job because of his race.

18 U.S.C. § 371: If two or more persons conspire either to commit any offense against the United States, or to defraud the United States, or any agency thereof in any manner or for any purpose, and one or more of such persons do any act to effect the object of the conspiracy, each shall be fined under this title or imprisoned not more than five years, or both.

Example: Employee A telephones Coworker B and asks him to "clock him in" when reporting to work the next day because he knows he'll be running late. Coworker B does so. Both Employee A and Coworker B have committed this crime.

18 U.S.C. § 372: If two or more persons in any State, Territory, Possession, or District conspire to prevent, by force, intimidation, or threat, any person from accepting or holding any office, trust, or place of confidence under the United States, or from discharging any duties thereof, or to induce by like means any officer of the United States to leave the place, where his duties as an officer are required to be performed, or to injure him in his person or property on account of his lawful discharge of the duties of his office, or while engaged in the lawful discharge thereof, or to injure his property so as to molest, interrupt, hinder, or impede him in the discharge of his official duties, each of such persons shall be fined under this title or imprisoned not more than six years, or both.

Example: Two employees get together and decide to leave threatening notes on the desk of a coworker with the intention of getting the coworker to resign.

18 U.S.C. § 641: Whoever embezzles, steals, purloins, or knowingly converts to his use or the use of another, or without authority, sells, conveys or disposes of any record, voucher, money, or thing of value of the United States or of any department or agency thereof, or any property made or being made under contract for the United States or any department or agency thereof; or

Whoever receives, conceals, or retains the same with intent to convert it to his use or gain, knowing it to have been embezzled, stolen, purloined or converted—

Shall be fined under this title or imprisoned not more than ten years, or both; but if the value of such property does not exceed the sum of $1,000, he shall be fined under this title or imprisoned not more than one year, or both.

Example: An employee takes a ream of paper from the supply next to the agency's copy machine for his daughter's use in school on her computer.

18 U.S.C. § 842: Whoever, being an officer, or employee of the United States or any department or agency thereof, or representing himself to be or assuming to act as such, under color or pretense of office or employment commits or attempts an act of extortion, shall be fined under this title or imprisoned not more than three years, or both; but if the amount so extorted or demanded does not exceed $1,000, he shall be fined under this title or imprisoned not more than one year, or both.

Example: A security office of the agency offers to tear up the traffic ticket he is writing for a citizen he has stopped for speeding on agency property if the citizen will share with him some of the donuts the citizen has in his car.

18 U.S.C. § 1001: (a) Except as otherwise provided in this section, whoever, in any matter within the jurisdiction of the executive, legislative, or judicial branch of the Government of the United States, knowingly and willfully—

(1) falsifies, conceals, or covers up by any trick, scheme, or device a material fact;

(2) makes any materially false, fictitious, or fraudulent statement or representation; or

(3) makes or uses any false writing or document knowing the same to contain any materially false, fictitious, or fraudulent statement or entry;

shall be fined under this title or imprisoned not more than 5 years, or both.

Example: An employee lies while testifying during an EEOC hearing (or when giving a deposition prior to the hearing).

18 U.S.C. § 1018: Whoever, being a public officer or other person authorized by any law of the United States to make or give a certificate or other writing, knowingly makes and delivers as true such a certificate or writing, containing any statement which he knows to be false, in a case where the punishment thereof is not elsewhere expressly provided by law, shall be fined under this title or imprisoned not more than one year, or both.

Example: A supervisor signs and thereby approves a subordinate's performance rating even though the supervisor knows that the description of the employee's accomplishments during the rating period is exaggerated and untrue.

18 U.S.C. § 1512: (2) Whoever uses physical force or the threat of physical force against any person, or attempts to do so, with intent to—

(A) influence, delay, or prevent the testimony of any person in an official proceeding;

(B) cause or induce any person to—

(i) withhold testimony, or withhold a record, document, or other object, from an official proceeding;

(ii) alter, destroy, mutilate, or conceal an object with intent to impair the integrity or availability of the object for use in an official proceeding;

(iii) evade legal process summoning that person to appear as a witness, or to produce a record, document, or other object, in an official proceeding; or

(iv) be absent from an official proceeding to which that person has been summoned by legal process shall be punished as provided in paragraph (3).

Example: An employee says to a coworker, "Hey, man, if you give a copy of that email I sent you to the EEO investigator, I'll kick your behind."

18 U.S.C. § 1519: Whoever knowingly alters, destroys, mutilates, conceals, covers up, falsifies, or makes a false entry in any record, document, or tangible object with the intent to impede, obstruct, or influence the investigation or proper administration of any matter within the jurisdiction of any department or agency of the United States or any case filed under title 11, or in relation to or contemplation of any such matter or case, shall be fined under this title, imprisoned not more than 20 years, or both.

Example: An employee submits a written discrimination complaint to her agency claiming that her supervisor tried to kiss her and touched her buttocks when no such events actually occurred, and the employee knows the statements are false.

18 U.S.C. § 1621: Whoever—

(1) having taken an oath before a competent tribunal, officer, or person, in any case in which a law of the United States authorizes an oath to be administered, that he will testify, declare, depose, or certify truly, or that any written testimony, declaration, deposition, or certificate by him subscribed, is true, willfully and contrary to such oath states or subscribes any material matter which he does not believe to be true; or

(2) in any declaration, certificate, verification, or statement under penalty of perjury as permitted under section 1746 of title 28, United States Code, willfully subscribes as true any material matter which he does not believe to be true;

is guilty of perjury and shall, except as otherwise expressly provided by law, be fined under this title or imprisoned not more than five years, or both. This section is applicable whether the statement or subscription is made within or without the United States.

Example: An employee lies at an MSPB hearing.

18 U.S.C. § 1622: Whoever procures another to commit any perjury is guilty of subornation of perjury, and shall be fined under this title or imprisoned not more than five years, or both.

Example: An employee attempts to convince a coworker to lie at an MSPB hearing.

18 U.S.C. § 1917: Whoever, being a member or employee of the United States Office of Personnel Management or an individual in the public service, willfully and corruptly—

(1) defeats, deceives, or obstructs an individual in respect of his right of examination according to the rules prescribed by the President under title 5 for the administration of the competitive service and the regulations prescribed by such Office under section 1302 (a) of title 5;

(2) falsely marks, grades, estimates, or reports on the examination or proper standing of an individual examined;

(3) makes a false representation concerning the mark, grade, estimate, or report on the examination or proper standing of an individual examined, or concerning the individual examined; or

(4) furnishes to an individual any special or secret information for the purpose of improving or injuring the prospects or chances of an individual examined, or to be examined, being appointed, employed, or promoted;

shall, for each offense, be fined under this title not less than $100 or imprisoned not less than ten days nor more than one year, or both.

Example: A senior manager gives one of his employees who has applied for a promotion a copy of the questions he will be asked by the interviewing panel who will rank and rate the employee for the promotion.

18 U.S.C. § 1920: Whoever knowingly and willfully falsifies, conceals, or covers up a material fact, or makes a false, fictitious, or fraudulent statement or representation, or makes or uses a false statement or report knowing the same to contain any false, fictitious, or fraudulent statement or entry in connection with the application for or receipt of compensation or other benefit or payment under subchapter I or III of chapter 81 of title 5, shall be guilty of perjury, and on conviction thereof shall be punished by a fine under this title, or by imprisonment for not more than 5 years, or both; but if the amount of the benefits falsely obtained does not exceed $1,000, such person shall be punished by a fine under this title, or by imprisonment for not more than 1 year, or both.

Example: The employee files a claim for an on-the-job injury even though he actually was injured while in a non-work status over the weekend.

18 U.S.C. § 707: Whoever, with intent to defraud, wears or displays the sign or emblem of the 4–H clubs, consisting of a green four-leaf clover with stem, and the letter H in white or gold on each leaflet, or any insignia in colorable imitation thereof, for the purpose of inducing the belief that he is a member of, associated with, or an agent or representative for the 4–H clubs; or

Whoever, whether an individual, partnership, corporation or association, other than the 4–H clubs and those duly authorized by them, the representatives of the United States Department of Agriculture, the land grant colleges, and persons authorized by the Secretary of Agriculture, uses, within the United States, such emblem or any sign, insignia, or symbol in colorable imitation thereof, or the words "4–H Club" or "4–H Clubs" or any combination of these or other words or characters in colorable imitation thereof—

Shall be fined under this title or imprisoned not more than six months, or both.

Example: An employee wears a T-shirt to work emblazoned with the emblem of a 4-H club and asks coworkers for donation to support 4-H even though he has no intention of donating the money collected to 4-H and doesn't know a sheep from a goat.

OK, maybe that last one was a bit of a stretch. However, at the least it should serve to show you that there are federal crimes you may never have dreamed existed, and with the help of a good legal counsel, you just might be able to identify some of the misconduct that is causing you problems as a federal crime for which imprisonment may be imposed, and thereby invoke the shortened notice period of the crime provision.

Keep in mind, also, the crime provision is not limited to the commission of a federal crime. ANY crime will do: state, local, as well as federal. In California, for example, by case law, the act of spitting on someone is an assault and battery, and you can be sentenced to jail for the crime of assault and battery. In a federal workplace located in California, an employee who spits on a coworker (or his boss or a member of the public) could find himself looking down the barrel of a crime provision shortened notice period. So be creative and look far and wide when attempting to identify misconduct that might constitute a crime under some statute somewhere.

How to Fire a Government Employee

After all of this, you are ready to propose your employee's removal from government. Although there's no specific regulatory way of doing it, here's a common approach that is both fair to the employee and protective of the federal workplace:

- Have the employee meet you in a neutral area such as a conference room (not your office).
- Have an agency attorney or human resources specialist accompany you to the meeting.
- If a union has represented the employee previously, then the union has to be notified of the meeting. Otherwise, the employee has no right to union representation and the union has no independent right to be in the meeting.

- Have a security officer either in the room or just outside, in case the employee becomes violent (you cannot predict who will become violent. Take no chances; do not bet your life that the employee will not become violent).
- Hand the employee the proposed removal letter, saying something like, "Bill, I've found it necessary to propose that you be relieved of duty with the agency. Deborah from Human Resources is here to answer any questions you might have. After your questions have been answered, you are to go with her and do what she tells you for the rest of the day."
- Leave the room.
- After answering any questions, the HR specialist escorts the employee back to his office to gather his personal possessions, and then escorts him to the entrance to the facility. The security officer stays close by. The employee turns over his agency credentials and any other agency property he has, such as a cell phone.
- Notify information technology that the employee's access to the agency's computer system is to be disabled immediately.
- Place the employee on the no-entrance list if you work in a secure building.
- Notify the employee's coworkers that they are not to allow the employee to enter the building and are to notify you or security if the employee is seen in the vicinity of the facility. Give them a 24-hour phone number to call if necessary.
- Explain the situation to you' supervisory colleagues. In fact, you may want to do this before you deliver the proposed removal.
- Explain the situation to your family. Give each of them that 24-hour phone number.

Oh, I can hear the push back now. "My goodness, Bill and Deb. This is way more than necessary. Most people are not violent. OPM says that normally we are supposed to keep employees in the workplace once a removal is proposed. My HR people can tell who is going to be violent and advise me what to do." Yeah, well, grow up. Recent studies from the Bureau of Labor Statistics reveal that every workday in America (Monday thru Friday), two people are killed by a co-worker. And many of those killings are caused by individuals who had no history of violence. We will concede that normally you do not have to take all these precautions. But how many times should you have done this stuff, and not done it, to have the result being a really bad day at work?

Do not risk your life unnecessarily. Take these minimal procedural steps and increase your odds dramatically that you will make it to retirement

The judicial tone regarding today's federal workplace: As you may have noticed, court opinions and philosophies change over time. Many years ago, some citizens of our country were considered to be property rather than individuals. Fortunately, the courts changed their collective minds and that is no longer the case. Public whippings and hangings used to be the norm, but now the courts have held both to be cruel and unusual punishment. More recently, a woman's right to an abortion was guaranteed by the Supreme Court, but there is a possibility that the Court may swing again and determine that there is no such inherent Constitutional right.

The law of the government's workplace also moves back and forth over time. For several years, MSPB was quick to dismiss a late-filed appeal even if the lateness was only a few days or even hours. That view changed several years ago, and late filings are now more likely to be accepted. Until recently, MSPB was likely to defer to the agency's penalty selection. Today, it is more likely to substitute its judgment for that of the agency officials and mitigate a penalty it finds to be too severe.

Some of these changes are the result of the Board being a political body. They are political in the sense that the members are selected by the President. As the philosophy of the White House changes, so does the philosophy of the Board. Agency officials should stay abreast of trends in agency decisions and modify their policies accordingly.

Even if you make a mistake, you don't necessarily lose the case: Prior to the Civil Service Reform Act of 1978 (CSRA), if an agency made an error in the handling of a termination action, the agency automatically lost and the employee got his job back. That all changed with the enactment of the CSRA. Today if a supervisor makes an inadvertent error when taking a disciplinary action, the action will be reversed only if the employee can prove that the error was harmful.

For example, in this section we have pressed for agencies to consider using the crime provision to shorten a notice period. However, just for the sake of speculation, let's say that the agency does so and on appeal, the court rules that the proposing supervisor failed to prove that he had "reasonable cause" to believe that the employee had committed a crime for which imprisonment could be imposed. In other words, the employee was entitled to a full 30 days of notice prior to termination and the agency gave only 7. It feels like this could be an easy win for the employee, doesn't it?

Well, it is not. Unless the employee can prove that the agency would have reached a different decision on the proposed discipline if there had been 30 days of notice rather than 7, the agency action will still be sustained even though it was improper for the agency to invoke the crime provision. The worst that will happen if the employee is able to prove that the agency made a harmless error by invoking the crime provision is that the agency will have to pay 21 days of back pay to make up for the difference between the notice period given and the notice period to which the employee was entitled. Even though this is an untested area, aggressive agencies should take great comfort in knowing that if they pursue the crime provision option, and are wrong, they really have not put much at stake and will probably not lose the action because of this procedural impropriety.

Finally, if you choose to invoke the crime provision, please do so with your eyes wide open to the fact that what we are advocating here is an enlargement of the existing body of case law, an enlargement in a manner that we think is consistent with the statute and for which the judicial temperament appears to be ripe. However, we can't assure you that the Board and the courts will uphold every attempt to use the shortened notice period for misconduct that is a crime which can result in incarceration, but we can tell you that is what the statute allows. You can't play good basketball if you don't commit a foul every now and then. Agencies will have to win some and perhaps lose some of these cases before we all know just how far this flexibility can be played.

INTERESTING ALTERNATIVES

There are a couple of aggressive options that have been suggested by recent Board and court decisions, but that we hesitate to recommend fully simply because we do not know just how far these can be pushed. We present them for you briefly here in the hopes that some hard-charging steely-eyed supervisor, with the help of an assertive, experienced support staff, will try these out and help develop the case law. Be sure to study the cases in depth before you get very far in these untested areas.

Hey, even if you lose, we'll all be very thankful that you tried.

Emergency Suspension as a Non-appealable Action

In *Bradley v. USPS,* AT-0752-03-0582-I-1 (July 23, 2004), the Postal Service placed Bradley in an off-duty non-pay status because he was acting in a manner that made the agency believe that he might be injurious to himself or others. Specifically, he cursed his supervisor, refused to obey direct orders, and dared his supervisor to hit him. The Postal Service specifically invoked a provision of its collective bargaining agreement to place Bradley in an "emergency suspension" status and to send him home without pay until it completed an investigation of the situation.

The Postal Service then subsequently suspended the employee using standard notice-response-suspension procedures, but that is not the most important part of the ruling in this case.

When Bradley appealed to the Merit System Protection Board, he argued that the emergency suspension was appealable to the Board and within its jurisdiction because he was deprived of a paycheck. However, the Board reasoned that it did not have jurisdiction over the emergency suspension because by law it has jurisdiction over suspensions of more than 14 days only when the placement of the employee in a non-duty non-pay status is for *disciplinary reasons* (5 U.S.C. § 7501(2)). By invoking the specific provision of the agency's collective bargaining agreement that allows for suspensions without pay for reasons relative to maintaining the safety of the workplace, the agency avoided suspending Bradley for disciplinary reasons and thereby avoided Board jurisdiction.

Wow. What a nice distinction. One of the huge problems in government today is the perception that employees behaving badly cannot be dealt with quickly and decisively. Some agencies, when confronted with the dangerous employee would have sent him home on investigative leave (i.e. with pay, but no duties) and have used that time to conduct an investigation and propose a disciplinary action. Others might not even have thought of the investigative leave option and may have left the employee on the job (and his coworkers in harm's way) until a disciplinary suspension or removal could be proposed. The Bradley case and others similar to it give agencies a significant tool that can be used immediately to deal with a potentially dangerous employee.

A key factor, however, appears to be that the agency had a formal policy in place before the disruptive event, and then specifically invoked that policy when placing the employee into a non-pay non-duty status for a non-disciplinary reason. Few agencies have policies such as this, perhaps because few agencies have had such tremendous problems with workplace violence as has the Postal Service. That means that for this to be a viable aggressive strategy, a policy providing for non-disciplinary suspensions should be put into place before it is needed.

So how does a supervisor put such a policy into place so it can be used in disruptive situations? Well, the Office of Personnel Management could amend the Code of Federal Regulations to make such an action a government-wide option for agencies covered under Title V of the United States Code. However, agencies need not wait for OPM to act. As the Postal Service did through collective bargaining, an agency head could establish an emergency suspension policy for the entire agency through the simple issuance of a written policy statement. Or, the head of a major agency subcomponent could issue such a policy. The regional director of a particular geographical area could do it or even the senior manager in a particular location or organizational component may be able to. In fact, the theory of discipline would suggest that a single supervisor could establish such a policy and enforce it by giving notice to employees of its existence prior to its enforcement.

In other words, in theory just about any level of supervision could establish an emergency suspension policy and avoid Board jurisdiction in situations similar to Bradley's. In practice, of course, this is such a significant issue, most agencies would probably deny individual supervisors the authority to come up with individual emergency suspension policies and might alternatively develop a comprehensive policy at a high level that could be enforced (and bargained with the union, as necessary) across a broad section of the agency.

Those readers of this book who are at a high level in an organization and in a position to influence agency policy would do the supervisors and managers of your organization a great service by developing and implementing a comprehensive emergency suspension policy similar to the one invoked by the Postal Service to immediately put Bradley on the beach for a couple of weeks without pay while it sorted things out and without invoking the jurisdiction of higher level review by MSPB.

Those readers who are lower in the organizational structure and who would like to be able to say to an offending employee, "I order you to leave the workplace immediately and not return until you are told to do so by me," may want to send your friends and contacts in higher positions a copy of this text with this particular section highlighted. Perhaps that'll get their attention enough to develop a policy for you.

Books make delightful holiday gifts, don't you think? And, the federal government has several such gift-giving holidays for which this book just might be the perfect present. Ethics rules regarding gifts? Never heard of them.

A Second Probationary Period for a Long-Term Employee

In *Shelton v. Air Force*, No. 04-3136 (Fed. Cir. Sep. 1, 2004), Shelton was employed by the Air Force for seven years, had a break in service of 13 years, and then was rehired by the Air Force into the same position.

Shelton had clearly completed the standard one-year probationary period when she was hired, and upon her re-employment, many agencies would have reinstated her as a career employee.

However, the Air Force did not see it to be that straightforward. It was concerned that Shelton may no longer have what it takes to be a government employee, so upon her reinstatement, she was informed that her appointment was "subject to the completion of a [new] one-year initial probationary period." Now, there's nothing in the regulations that says that an agency can do this; the Air Force, to its great credit, just decided that it made sense from a management standpoint, and did it.

Unfortunately, poor Shelton was not able to perform up to the agency's standards during her first year of re-employment, and she was separated during probation. She appealed to MSPB and then to court arguing that she completed her initial probationary period way back in the early 80's and that the Air Force was without the authority to impose yet another probationary period on her. Both the Board and the court held that she could not appeal her termination, that she was indeed serving in a probationary period, and that the Air Force's "imposition of a reasonable condition to accommodate a special circumstance is not an illegal employment action."

So just what do we have here? Well, the only case that the court mentioned that was used for authority by the agency was a different situation where the referenced employee was hired from an Office of Personnel Management "certificate." It has long been held that hiring an individual from an OPM certificate begins a new probationary period, even if the employee has many years of prior government service. Therefore, we have no authority or rationale beyond what the court said in its decision.

In abbreviated form, the court seemed impressed by the following factors:

- The break in service was long – 13 years.
- The Air Force told Shelton when she was being re-hired that the probationary period would be in effect, thereby making Shelton's acceptance of the appointment under those terms voluntary.
- The Air Force's action was otherwise "reasonable."

Long term practitioners who read this decision will start to think of a variety of interesting permutations of the court's logic:

- If a 13-year break in service warrants a new probationary period, surely a 10-year break would as well. And maybe even a five-year or a three. We won't know where the bottom end of this range is until we see more cases.
- The Air Force told Shelton, "Hey, if you want this job, it comes with a new probationary period. Take it or leave it." When a job applicant/selectee acquiesces to a condition of employment by accepting the job offer with full knowledge of the condition, rather than having it unilaterally forced upon him after acceptance of an appointment, the court appears to believe that makes the condition acceptable.
- The court upheld the agency's action because it was "reasonable" even though there was no specific regulatory or statutory authority empowering the agency to do what it did. Could this be the beginning of the court's allowing government agencies to create their own "reasonable" flexibilities unless the regulatory system expressly prohibits the flexibility? If so, we could be in for a whole new world of agency experimentation.

We hesitate to speculate too much about what this decision means, and our examples here are a bit stretched. However, the fundamental shift in the court's apparent logic when it comes to dealing with agency authority that appears to be embodied in the Shelton decision could allow agencies to do things never dreamed of before. At a minimum, OPM as the leader, or agencies acting individually, should start to consider establishing policies that specifically allow for probationary periods beyond the initial period in cases in which the break in service is long.

Lower Burden of Proof for Lesser Disciplinary Actions

This one is for you policy makers out there. For many years, the accepted burdens of evidentiary proof have been:

- A preponderance of the evidence for disciplinary actions (i.e., it probably happened)
- Substantial evidence for unacceptable performance actions (i.e., it might have happened)

We find the preponderance standard articulated in regulation at 5 CFR 1201.4(q), and the substantial standard articulated by regulation at 5 CFR 1201.4(p). However, these regulations apply only to matters appealable to MSPB: suspensions of more than 14 days, demotions, and removals. There is no regulation nor statute that defines the burden of proof that an agency must satisfy to suspend an employee for 14 days or fewer or to issue a Reprimand.

Most all civil service law practitioners have acted on the premise that a preponderance of evidence is required for short suspensions because a preponderance of evidence is required for long (appealable to MSPB) suspensions. However, when you really read the regulations and law closely, you find no regulatory support for that conclusion.

Congress recently has lowered the burden of proof for all adverse actions taken at the VA to the substantial level. That action reminds us that there is no inherent reason that discipline for misconduct has to be proven at the preponderance level. Therefore, it would seem that an agency by policy could set the burden of proof for reprimands and suspensions of 14 days or fewer at the substantial level.

Avoid Suspensions Entirely

If we were writing a discipline policy for an agency, we would do away with suspensions altogether. First, there's no evidence that a suspension is more likely to correct bad behavior than a disciplinary action that does not deprive the employee of part of his salary. Second, when a supervisor suspends an employee, the suspension often harms the agency more than the employee:

- We have heard of supervisors having to pay thousands of dollars in overtime to get the work done that the suspended employee cannot.
- Alternatively, the work not performed by the suspended employee is reassigned to already overworked coworkers, thereby causing them resentment.
- Or, perhaps the work simply doesn't get done or is performed by the supervisor himself.

A suspension for misconduct serves two purposes: to motivate the employee to obey workplace rules and to lay a foundation in progressive discipline should the employee engage in a future act of misconduct. What if there was a disciplinary tool for the supervisor that could accomplish both of these objectives while simultaneously avoiding the significant harm caused an agency by a suspension? Wouldn't that be great?

Fortunately, there is: a Reprimand in Lieu of a Suspension. Here's how it works:

1. The supervisor proposes a 1 to 14-day suspension.
2. The employee responds.
3. The Deciding Official makes the employee an offer:
   a. He tells the employee that discipline is definitely warranted.
   b. He then tells the employee he would like to avoid taking away part of the employee's paycheck by suspending him.
   c. Finally, he tells the employee that if he will accept a Reprimand in Lieu of a Suspension, acknowledge that it carries the weight of a suspension for the purpose of progressive discipline, and waive his rights to file a grievance or complaint, then that will be that.

If the employee declines the offer, then the supervisor is left with the proposed suspension to decide. However, it will be the rare employee who would rather lose a few days of pay than accept a lesser punishment.

We know that this approach works, that having the employee voluntarily accept a Reprimand in Lieu of a Suspension counts toward progressive discipline, because MSPB has ruled favorably in cases in which agencies have done this. However, with one exception, we have no case law that says one way or the other that an agency's unilateral imposition of a Reprimand in Lieu of a Suspension without the employee's consent counts as equivalent to a prior suspension. The exception is in discipline that occurs in the US Postal Service. Through collective bargaining, management and the union have included this tool in the collective bargaining agreement. It is conceivable that MSPB might rule in the future that a unilaterally imposed Reprimand in Lieu of a Suspension somehow deprives the employee of the negative reinforcement benefit of a lost-pay suspension.

The way to avoid this possibility would be to rewrite the agency's discipline policy to foreclose the use of suspensions altogether. Simply say that a first offence of misconduct warrants a Reprimand, a second offense of Misconduct warrants a Reprimand in Lieu of a Suspension (or "Final Reprimand"), and that a third offense of misconduct warrants removal. MSPB does not have the authority to overrule an agency's discipline policy. A policy change would guarantee that the Board could not rule that the supervisor has somehow denied the employee the "benefit" of a suspension. The unilateral imposition of any disciplinary action can be challenged by the employee through a complaint or grievance. A policy change has this disadvantage as compared to the option in which the employee negotiates to avoid a suspension.

CHAPTER 8
CONCLUSION

In these pages, we have attempted to help you understand the basic principles of dealing with a problem employee in a government organization. We have covered how to sort out the status of the employee early on so that you will know the options open to you for action. We have laid out the five fundamental elements of every misconduct action and compared them to the four fundamental elements of every unacceptable performance action. We have given you the details of the termination process itself, and then rounded out our discussion by covering some of the tricks of the trade when confronted with special challenges and when seeking to use aggressive strategies.

Quite frankly, as we said at the beginning of this book, we hope you never need to use this book at all. If our hiring processes were perfect and our management styles always effective, we might never have to fire any government employee. Unfortunately, we are not at that point yet, and until we get there, there will always be government employees who do not deserve a pay check. As a government supervisor, it is your responsibility to make sure that such employees are terminated from their positions of public trust, and government functions are made as civil as we can make them.

The following examples demonstrate the documents you might use to remove a government employee from employment. The first few documents are examples of the sorts of documents you would create in a misconduct situation, followed by a "Last Rites" agreement that memorializes the employee's voluntary resignation/retirement in exchange for consideration by the supervisor. The documents beyond the "Agency Supported Job Search Agreement" are used specifically for other situations in which the employee agrees to do something in exchange for the supervisor not invoking the traditional discipline of a suspension or removal. And finally, the Appendix ends with a couple of documents you would use if the problem is unacceptable performance rather than misconduct.

Yes, it really can be this simple. From your authors, we wish you the best of luck. If we can ever be of assistance, fell free to contact us: Wiley@FELTG.com or Hopkins@FELTG.com

APPENDIX

From: Sam Supervisor [mailto:sam@thisagency.gov]

Sent: Thursday, March 07, 20XX 10:02 AM

To: Ed Employee

Subj: Time, attendance and leave policy

As a reminder, these are the time, attendance, and leave rules for our office:

- Work hours are 8:00 AM to 4:30 PM Monday through Friday.
- Our lunch break is from Noon to 12:30 PM daily.
- Requests for leave and variations to the above schedule must be made to me personally, by phone or email, in advance of any absences, except in emergency situations.

If you have any questions, please let me know immediately.

Sam

Sam Supervisor
Head, Administrative Division, Administrative and Logistics Department
(202) 653-6772

This email establishes the rule with which the employee must comply and simultaneously puts the employee on notice of the rule, thereby satisfying Elements One and Two of the five elements of discipline (see Chapter Two).

U.S. ADMINISTRATIVE SERVICES AGENCY
1600 J STREET NW
WASHINGTON, DC 20013

From: Sam Supervisor, Head, Administrative Division, Administrative and Logistics Department

To: Ed Employee, Project Clerk, GS-303-9

Subj: Reprimand

Date: March 14, 20XX

By this letter I am reprimanding you for the following misconduct and warning you that if you repeat this or other misconduct, you may be suspended or removed:

> On March 7, 20XX, I informed you that the lunch break period for our office is from noon to 12:30. Yesterday, I observed you leaving your desk at 11:40 AM to go to lunch and not returning until 1:00 PM.

A copy of this reprimand will remain in your Official Personnel Folder for up to two years. During this time, I will consider it a prior act of discipline should you again engage in further misconduct.

Should you so choose, you have the right to dispute this reprimand by filing an administrative grievance with Branch Chief Margaret Manager by March 28, 201X. For information as to this and other rights you might have, you may consult with Hank Richards in Human Resources, (202) 653-6772.

____

[Supervisor's signature]

If the employee is in a collective bargaining unit, in this and the other letters in this collection, he should be given information as to how to file a grievance under the negotiated grievance procedure. In addition, some practitioners choose to include notification to the employee of additional rights such as to file a discrimination complaint or to seek employee assistance counseling, and a place for the employee to sign as having received the letter. These are unnecessary inclusions. We suggest you avoid them.

The supervisor's observation satisfies Element Three of the five elements of discipline.

U.S. Administrative Services Agency
1600 J Street NW
Washington, DC 20013

From: Sam Supervisor, Head, Administrative Division, Administrative and Logistics Department

To: Ed Employee, Project Clerk, GS-303-9

Subj: Proposed Suspension

Date: April 15, 20XX

By this letter I am proposing that you be suspended without pay for two days for the following misconduct:

> On March 7, 20XX, I informed you that the lunch break period for our office is from noon to 12:30. Yesterday, I observed you leaving your desk to go to lunch at 11:50 AM and not returning until 1:45 PM.

In selecting this penalty, I note that I reprimanded you for similar misconduct on March 14, 20XX.

You have the right to respond to this proposal in writing and in person with Branch Chief Margaret Manager. If you choose to exercise this right, you may meet with Branch Chief Manager at 10:00 AM on April 17, 20XX in the main conference room, Building 123. For information as to this and other rights you might have, you may consult with Hank Richards in Human Resources, (202) 653-6772.

____

[Supervisor's signature]

[Regulatory Note: Congress has passed a recent law that requires OPM to draft language to be included in proposed discipline letters explaining to the employee what the appeal rights will be should the proposed action be implemented. Unfortunately, as of this printing, OPM has not yet developed that language. Be sure to rely on your advisors as to what that language should be used once it is developed. Fortunately, if you by mistake fail to include that language, it should not cause your proposal to be set aside on appeal as it would be difficult to conclude that such an omission was a "harmful error."]

U.S. Administrative Services Agency
1600 J Street NW
Washington, DC 20013

From: Margaret Manager, Chief, Administrative and Logistics Department

To: Ed Employee, Project Clerk, GS-303-9

Subj: Decision Regarding Proposed Suspension

Date: April 17, 20XX

On April 15, 20XX, Sam Supervisor proposed to me that you be suspended without pay for two days based on the following misconduct:

> On March 7, 20XX, Mr. Supervisor informed you that the lunch break period for your office is from noon to 12:30. On April 14, 20XX, Mr. Supervisor observed you leaving your desk at 11:50 AM and not returning until 1:45 PM.

On April 17, 20XX, you responded to me orally regarding this proposal, stating that you did not believe your absence was significant. In consideration of the proposal and your response, I conclude that a two-day suspension is warranted for your act of misconduct. You are hereby suspended without pay on April 18 and 19, 20XX. You are not to report to work these dates. Should you repeat this or other misconduct, you may be suspended for a greater period of time or removed

You have the right to dispute this suspension by filing an administrative grievance with Director Charles Executive by April 30, 20XX. For information as to this and other rights you might have, you may consult with Hank Richards in Human Resources, (202) 653-6772.

____

[Manager's signature]

[Reprimand in Lieu of a Suspension]

U.S. Administrative Services Agency
1600 J Street NW
Washington, DC 20013

From: Sam Supervisor, Head, Administrative Division, Administrative and Logistics Department

To: Ed Employee, Project Clerk, GS-303-9

Subj: Proposed Suspension

Date: April 15, 20XX

By this letter I am proposing that you be suspended without pay for two days for the following misconduct:

> On March 7, 20XX, I informed you that the lunch break period for our office is from noon to 12:30. Yesterday, I observed you leaving your desk to go to lunch at 11:50 AM and not returning until 1:45 PM.

In selecting this penalty, I note that I reprimanded you for similar misconduct on March 14, 20XX.

You have the right to respond to this proposal in writing and in person with Branch Chief Margaret Manager. If you choose to exercise this right, you may meet with Branch Chief Manager at 10:00 AM on April 17, 20XX in the main conference room, Building 123. For information as to this and other rights you might have, you may consult with Hank Richards in Human Resources, (202) 653-6772.

____

[Supervisor's signature]

By my signature below, I accept responsibility for this act of misconduct, acknowledge that discipline is warranted, and accept a Reprimand in Lieu of a Suspension as an alternative form of discipline. I understand that the agency will consider this Reprimand in Lieu of a Suspension equivalent to the proposed suspension for the purpose of progressive discipline should I engage in future misconduct. Finally, I hereby waive my rights to challenge this action in any manner or forum.

____

Ed Employee *Date*

U.S. Administrative Services Agency
1600 J Street NW
Washington, DC 20013

From: Sam Supervisor, Head, Administrative Division, Administrative and Logistics Department

To: Ed Employee, Project Clerk, GS-303-9

Subj: Proposed Removal

Date: July 9, 20XX

By this letter I am proposing that you be removed from employment for the following misconduct:

> **Charge - AWOL:** You did not report to work on July 5 or 8, 20XX, and you did not notify me in advance nor otherwise request leave for these absences. I have charged you 16 hours of Absent Without Leave for these dates.

In selecting this penalty, I relied on the penalty selection factors as described in the attached Douglas Factor Worksheet.

You have the right to be represented and to respond to this proposal in writing and orally with Branch Chief Margaret Manager. If you choose to exercise the right to respond in writing, you should submit those documents to Branch Chief Manager so that they are received no later than July 16, 20XX. If you choose to respond to this proposal orally, you may do so by calling Branch Chief Manager at 10:00 AM on July 17, 20XX. The contact information for your responses is:

> Margaret Manager, Branch Chief, Administrative and Logistics Department
> U.S. Administrative Services Agency
> 1600 J Street NW
> Washington, DC 20013
> (202) 653-6773 voice; (202) 653-6774 fax
> mmanager@usasa.gov

I will maintain you in a regular pay status from today until the date of the decision. However, I have determined that allowing you to remain in the workplace jeopardizes a government interest. Therefore, you are not to report to the worksite and you will be carried on paid Notice Leave until further notice. You are to immediately surrender all agency property in your possession, including your government credentials. In addition, you are to remove all personal property from your work space today.

The documents I have relied on in making this proposal are attached to this memo. For information as to this proposal, you may consult with Hank Richards in Human Resources, (202) 653-6772.

____

[Supervisor's signature]

DOUGLAS FACTOR WORKSHEET
Factors Relevant to the Proposed Penalty
Douglas v. Veterans Administration, 5 MSPR 280 (1981)

Name of Employee: Ed Employee
Position: Project Clerk, GS-303-9

By my signature below, under penalty of perjury, I hereby swear that I have considered the following factors in the manner indicated when selecting a penalty in this case:

1. The nature and seriousness of the offense and its relation to the employee's duties, position, and responsibilities, including whether the offense was intentional or technical or inadvertent, or was committed maliciously or for gain, or was frequently repeated:

> **Response:** *Unjustified absences from work without prior approval strike at the heart of the employer-employee relationship. Mr. Employee's absence caused another employee's leave to be cancelled and the delay of the office's budget submission by a week.*

2. The employee's job level and type of employment, including supervisory or fiduciary role, contacts with the public, and prominence of the position:

3. The employee's past disciplinary record:

> **Response:** *Within the past six months, Mr. Employee has received a reprimand and a second suspension of two days, all for attendance-related misconduct.*

4. The employees past work record, including length of government service, performance on the job, ability to get along with coworkers, and dependability:

> **Response:** *Mr. Edwards has worked for the agency for five years. He has no other government employment history. His performance ratings have been above average to Outstanding.*

5. The effect of the offense upon the employee's ability to perform at a satisfactory level and its effect upon the supervisor's confidence in the employee's ability to perform assigned duties:

> **Response:** *I have lost confidence in Mr. Employee's ability to maintain a consistent work schedule.*

6. Consistency of the penalty with those imposed upon other employees for the same or similar offenses:

> **Response:** *I know of no other employees in the Administrative and Logistics Division who have engaged in repeated acts of misconduct similar to this.*

7. Consistency of the penalty with applicable agency table of penalties:

8. The notoriety of the offense or its impact upon the reputation of the agency:

9. The clarity with which the employee was put on notice of any rules that were violated in committing the offense or had been warned about the offense in question:

> **Response:** *On March 7, 20XX, I informed Mr. Employee by email that he is to request leave from me prior to any absences. That notice was both specific and recent.*

10. The potential for the employee's rehabilitation:

> **Response:** *Repeated acts of misconduct which have been disciplined suggest a poor potential for rehabilitation. In addition, Mr. Employee has stated that he does not believe he had to conform with my rules because other offices did not have similar policies.*

11. Mitigating circumstances surrounding the offense such as unusual job tensions, personality problems, mental impairment, harassment, or bad faith, malice, or provocation on the part of others involved in the matter:

Response: *Mr. Employee claims that he has been under a lot of stress at home lately.*

12. The adequacy and effectiveness of alternative sanctions to deter such conduct in the future by the employee or others:

Response: *I have considered lesser penalties and determined that none would be effective in correcting the misconduct.*

PENALTY SELECTED: *Removal*

____

(Supervisor's Signature)

[Regulatory Note: Congress has passed a recent law that requires OPM to draft language to be included in proposed discipline letters explaining to the employee what the appeal rights will be should the proposed action be implemented. Unfortunately, as of this printing, OPM has not yet developed that language. Be sure to rely on your advisors as to what that language should be once it is developed. Fortunately, if you by mistake fail to include that language, it should not cause your proposal to be set aside on appeal as it would be difficult to conclude that such an omission was a "harmful error."]

U.S. Administrative Services Agency
1600 J Street NW
Washington, DC 20013

From: Margaret Manager, Branch Chief, Administrative and Logistics Department

To: Ed Employee, Project Clerk, GS-303-9

Subj: Decision Regarding Proposed Removal

Date: July 18, 20XX

On July 9, 20XX, Sam Supervisor proposed to me that you be removed from employment. You responded to me orally and in writing regarding this proposal. In your response you stated that you feel you are being discriminated against because of your sex and age, and that you are being reprised against because you are a whistleblower. However, you presented no evidence to support your claims of unfair treatment. Otherwise, you do not deny your absence or your failure to request leave. Therefore, I conclude that the misconduct occurred as charged.

Penalty: In selecting a penalty, I have considered those factors identified in the proposal, as well as your refusal to accept responsibility for your actions in your response to the proposal. Therefore, I conclude that your removal is warranted to be effective August 10, 20XX.

Rights: You have the right to appeal this decision to the U.S. Merit Systems Protection Board. An appeal must be filed no later than 30 days after today, or 30 days after the date of receipt of this decision, whichever is later. The address for filing an appeal is U.S. MSPB, Washington Regional Office, 1800 Diagonal Road, Alexandria, Virginia 22314. An appeal form is attached. MSPB's regulations and the on-line e-appeal option may be found at www.mspb.gov. If you do decide to file an appeal with MSPB, you should notify the Board that the agency contact official for the purpose of your appeal is:

Hank Richards, Senior Human Resources Specialist
U.S. Administrative Services Agency
1600 J Street NW
Washington, DC 20013
Telephone (202) 653-6773; fax (202) 653-6774;
hrichards@asa.gov

Or, you may seek corrective action before the U.S. Office of Special Counsel, www.osc.gov. However, if you do so, your appeal will be limited to whether the agency removed you in retaliation for making protected whistleblowing disclosures. You will be forgoing the right to otherwise challenge this removal. Finally, you have the right to file a complaint with the U.S. Equal Employment Opportunity Commission consistent with the provisions of 5 U.S.C. 7121(d) and 29 CFR 1614.301 and 1614.302, www.eeoc.gov.

____

[Manager's signature]

U.S. Administrative Services Agency
1600 J Street NW
Washington, DC 20013

From: Sam Supervisor, Head, Administrative Division, Administrative and Logistics Department

To: Ed Employee, Project Clerk, GS-303-9

Subj: Performance Demonstration Period Initiation

Date: March 1, 20XX

By this memo I am initiating a performance Demonstration Period (DP) to give you the opportunity to demonstrate acceptable performance. I have determined that your performance on Critical Element(s) [insert number(s)] of the attached performance plan is at the Unacceptable level. Should you fail to raise your level of performance above the unacceptable level during the DP, I am required to initiate steps to remove you from your position. The DP begins today and ends no later than April 1, 20XX. If you make more than two errors during this 30-day period, your performance will warrant a rating of Unacceptable and your removal from your position.

Additional Information Regarding the Critical Element(s):

> [It is not mandatory that you explain the standards more than they are explained in the performance plan. However, many critical elements are not written with the precision and specificity required by law. Take this opportunity to state in clear detail (to "flesh out" the standard) what performance is expected and how it will be measured. It is better NOT to reference specific prior shortcomings as doing so makes the employee defensive and tends to focus the employee on the past rather than the critical future.]

During the DP, I am responsible for assisting you to reach an acceptable level of performance. You are to address any questions, confusion, or problems to me immediately when they occur. In addition, you are to attend a weekly meeting with me, scheduled for 2:00 PM each Friday in my office during the DP to discuss your performance for the week. At our first meeting this Friday, you are to bring with you the following:

Firm Benchmarks of Expectation

> [Specify work products related to the critical element(s) at issue that the employee should be able to produce by the first meeting; e.g., a list of all projects currently pending with projected completion dates, an outline of a plan for dealing with an upcoming assignment, etc. Requiring similar assignments be produced at every weekly meeting provides a good opportunity for constructive feedback and documents performance for the week.]

U.S. ADMINISTRATIVE SERVICES AGENCY
1600 J STREET NW
WASHINGTON, DC 20013

From: Sam Supervisor, Head, Administrative Division, Administrative and Logistics Department

To: Ed Employee, Project Clerk, GS-303-9

Subj: Performance Demonstration Period Completion and Warning

Date: April 2, 20XX

By this letter I am pleased to inform you that you have successfully completed the performance Demonstration Period I initiated on March 1, 20XX. You are now performing at an acceptable level. However, be aware that should your performance again become unacceptable on Critical Element(s) [insert number(s)] between now and March 1, 20XY, I will immediately initiate steps to remove you from your position.

____

[Supervisor's signature]

U.S. Administrative Services Agency
1600 J Street NW
Washington, DC 20013

From: Sam Supervisor, Head, Administrative Division, Administrative and Logistics Department

To: Ed Employee, Project Clerk, GS-303-9

Subj: Proposed Removal for Unacceptable Performance

Date: April 2, 20XX

On March 1, 20XX, I initiated a performance Demonstration Period to allow you an opportunity period to demonstrate whether you could perform acceptably. By this letter I am proposing that you be removed from employment for the following incidents of unacceptable performance that occurred during this period relative to critical element 2 of the attached performance plan:

1. On March 4, 20XX, I assigned you the task to provide me a summary of all pending work assigned to you by March 8. You did not provide me that summary by March 8.
2. On March 8, 20XX, I directed you to draft the XYZ report in the format contained in our standard operating procedures. The draft you provided was not consistent with our standard format in that it did not contain an executive summary, table of contents, or index.
3. On March 22, 20XX, I directed you to coordinate with the head of the Logistics Department to arrange for getting information from that office in a timely manner. I told you to do this by March 29, 20XX, but you did not make this contact.

You have the right to be represented and to respond to this proposal in writing and orally with Branch Chief Margaret Manager. If you choose to exercise the right to respond in writing, you should submit those documents to Branch Chief Manager so that they are received no later than April 10, 20XX. If you choose to respond to this proposal orally, you may do so by calling Branch Chief Manager at 10:00 AM on April 11, 20XX. The contact information for your responses is:

> Margaret Manager, Branch Chief, Administrative and Logistics Department
> U.S. Administrative Services Agency
> 1600 J Street NW
> Washington, DC 20013
> (202) 653-6773 voice; (202) 653-6774 fax; mmanager@usasa.gov

I will maintain you in a regular pay status from today until the date of the decision. However, I have determined that allowing you to remain in the workplace jeopardizes a government interest. Therefore, you are not to report to the worksite and you will be carried on paid Notice Leave until further notice. You are to immediately surrender all agency property in your possession, including your government credentials. In addition, you are to remove all personal property from your work space today.

The documents I have relied on in making this proposal are attached to this memo. For information as to this proposal, you may consult with Hank Richards in Human Resources, (202) 653-6772.

____

[Supervisor's signature]

U.S. Administrative Services Agency
1600 J Street NW
Washington, DC 20013

From: Margaret Manager, Branch Chief, Administrative and Logistics Department

To: Ed Employee, Project Clerk, GS-303-9

Subj: Decision Regarding Proposed Removal for Unacceptable Performance

Date: May 3, 20XX

On April 2, 20XX, Sam Supervisor proposed to me that you be removed from employment based on three incidents of unacceptable performance that occurred during your performance Demonstration Period from March 1 through April 1, 20XX.

On April 11, 20XX, you responded to me orally and in writing regarding this proposal. In your response you stated that you were overworked during this period and that it was impossible for you to complete the three failed assignments you were given. In addition, you stated that you have not been trained in the proper format for preparing reports.

I have considered your responses and it is my conclusion that the three incidents of unacceptable performance occurred as described in the proposal letter, and that your reasons for failing to complete the assignments do not excuse your unacceptable performance. Therefore, it is my determination that your removal from service is warranted, effective today, May 3, 20XX.

Rights: You have the right to appeal this decision to the U.S. Merit Systems Protection Board. An appeal must be filed no later than 30 days after today, or 30 days after the date of receipt of this decision, whichever is later. The address for filing an appeal is U.S. MSPB, Washington Regional Office, 1800 Diagonal Road, Alexandria, Virginia 22314. An appeal form is attached. MSPB's regulations and the on-line e-appeal option may be found at www.mspb.gov. If you do decide to file an appeal with MSPB, you should notify the Board that the agency contact official for the purpose of your appeal is:

Hank Richards, Senior Human Resources Specialist
U.S. Administrative Services Agency
1600 J Street NW
Washington, DC 20013
Telephone (202) 653-6773; FAX (202) 653-6774;
Richards@asa.gov

Or, you may seek corrective action before the U.S. Office of Special Counsel, www.osc.gov. However, if you do so, your appeal will be limited to whether the agency took one or more covered personnel actions against you in retaliation for making protected whistleblowing disclosures. You will be forgoing the right to otherwise challenge this removal. Finally, you have the right to file a complaint with the U.S. Equal Employment Opportunity Commission consistent with the provisions of 5 U.S.C. 7121(d) and 29 CFR 1614.301 and 1614.302, www.eeoc.gov.

____

[Manager's signature]

Agency-Supported Job Search Agreement

This agreement is entered into voluntarily to provide the below-signed employee the opportunity to secure other employment with the support of the agency. For a 60-day period beginning on the date this agreement is executed, the agency agrees to work from home while seeking other employment. In this status, the employee will receive full pay, will be assigned little work, and will not report to the work site to allow the employee time to engage in a job search for another position. In exchange, the employee agrees to resign voluntarily effective the date this 60-day period expires if other employment has been secured by that time, and to refrain from challenging his removal should it occur.

The employee and the agency representative acknowledge that these commitments are irrevocable, that the agreement is considered executed on the date completely signed, and that the parties have had adequate time to consider this matter and to seek advice.

____________________________________ ___________________

[Employee's name] Date

____________________________________ ___________________

[Agency representative's name and title] Date

This is NOT a document required for removal. Rather, it is a "last rites" document embodying an agreement that would foreclose the need for the agency to purse removal and defend an appeal.

If the employee is 40 years old or older, add a paragraph to conform with the Older Worker Benefits Protection Act, 29 USC § 626(f) as follows:

> **Older Worker Benefits Protection Act:** By entering into this agreement, the employee is waiving rights contained in the Older Worker Benefits Protection Act (OWBPA) to allege age discrimination relative to this agreement, and is hereby advised to seek legal counsel prior to executing the agreement. The employee has up to 21 days to consider this proposal, and may rescind the agreement within a 7-day period after execution.

Last Chance Agreement

The agency has determined that the below-signed employee's conduct or performance warrants removal from employment. However, to allow the employee one final opportunity to demonstrate acceptable performance and conduct, the agency agrees to hold the implementation of the decision to remove in abeyance for a two-year period, beginning on the date of the last signature below.

During this period, the employee agrees to abide by all workplace rules and to perform at an acceptable level of performance on all critical elements. In exchange, the agency agrees to cancel its decision to remove the employee at the end of the period if the employee is successful. However, should the employee engage in future misconduct or unacceptable performance, the agency may take immediate steps to remove the employee. If this occurs, the employee agrees to waive all rights of any nature to challenge that decision through grievance or appeal.

The employee and the agency representative acknowledge that these commitments are irrevocable, that the agreement is considered executed on the date completely signed, and that the parties have had adequate time to consider this matter and to seek advice.

____

[Employee's name] Date

____

[Agency representative's name and title] Date

[If the employee is 40 years old or older, the agency will want to include the standard OWBPA language.]

Alternative to Discipline Agreement

The agency has determined that the below-signed employee's conduct warrants a two-day suspension from employment. However, to allow the employee the opportunity to correct behavior without being formally suspended, the agency agrees to cancel the proposed suspension in exchange for the following promises. The employee agrees to:

1. Donate eight hours of annual leave to the employee leave bank.

2. Perform eight hours of community service by volunteering to work as a math tutor for disadvantaged students at a local public school.

3 Accept responsibility for his actions and acknowledge that any future act of misconduct within two years from the signing of this agreement may warrant removal.

4. Waive all rights of any nature to challenge this action through appeal, grievance, complaint, or other administrative or judicial action.

The employee and the agency representative acknowledge that these commitments are irrevocable, that the agreement is considered executed on the date completely signed, and that the parties have had adequate time to consider this matter and to seek advice.

____

[Employee's name] Date

____

[Agency representative's name and title] Date

[If the employee is 40 years old or older, the agency will want to include the standard OWBPA language.]

How to Draft a Powerful Critical Element

Step 1. Using the employee's Position Description, list all tasks required to be performed.

Example: *Marine Biologist GS-0401-13*

1. Provides access, as appropriate, to offshore energy and marine mineral resources.
2. Oversees the environmentally sound development of these resources.
3. Coordinates the review and analysis of offshore energy and marine mineral lease proposals.
4. Managed the Financial Accountability and-Risk Management (FARM) Program.
5. Administers lease adjudication and management functions.
6. Conducts environmental reviews, analyses and consultations for proposed activities.
7. Ensuring compliance with environmental conditions of project approvals.
8. Plans and manages the Region's Environmental Studies Program (ESP).
9. Carries out the Region's Environmental analysis.
10. Conducts studies and pre- and post-lease evaluations.
11. Identifies important Regional and National data gaps and plans and oversees environmental studies contracts to satisfy regional and national information needs.
12. Contributes to the annual budget recommendation for Pacific OCS Region studies.
13. Contributes to the long-range planning of regional environmental information needs to meet OCS program objectives.
14. Identifies information needs and data gaps relative to oil and gas, renewable energy and marine mineral project.
15. Contributes to the annual Regional Studies Development Plan.
16. Plans for contracted environmental studies to obtain the required information including preparation of statements of work.
17. Manages contracted studies as the Contracting Officer's Representative (COR) and/or project inspector ·including the review of. draft reports; and disseminating the results of contracted environmental studies.
18. Works with the ESS chief to develop Regional Studies Development Plan and schedule and works with the ESS Chief in determining staff COR project assignments.
19. Plans and develops environmental studies in the field of marine ecology and marine biology to monitor offshore oil and gas activities or understand possible effects on multiple species, their interactions, and the ecosystems involved from offshore energy and marine mineral projects.
20. Provides technical support to the staff and management of the Pacific OCS Region and other AGENCY offices as appropriate regarding the professional specialties of marine ecology, fish resources, and fisheries.

Step 2. Cull the tasks so that you are left with only important tasks.

Important Tasks:

1. Provides access, as appropriate, to offshore energy and marine mineral resources.
2. Oversees the environmentally sound development of these resources.
3. Coordinates the review and analysis of offshore energy and marine mineral lease proposals.
4. Managed the Financial Accountability and-Risk Management (FARM) Program.
5. Administers lease adjudication and management functions.
6. Conducts environmental reviews, analyses and consultations for proposed activities.
7. Ensuring compliance with environmental conditions of project approvals.
8. Plans and manages the Region's Environmental Studies Program (ESP).
9. Carries out the Region's Environmental analysis.
10. Conducts studies and pre- and post-lease evaluations.

Step 3. Entitle a Critical Element as "Technical Expectations." Begin the description of the Fully Successful level of performance as follows:

> "Performs all of the following tasks within established time limits, consistent with accepted practices in the field, and free of any errors in the final product."

Then, use the tasks as sorted above as the Fully Successful level of performance.

Step 4. Define the other four levels of performance expectation as follows:

Exceptional	Performs at the Superior level, and in addition develops creative solutions for difficult challenges that arise during the appraisal period.
Superior	Performs all tasks as identified for the Fully Successful level, and in addition exhibits an overall degree of professionalism above that expected for the Fully Successful level.
Minimally Successful	Performs any task in a manner inconsistent with the expectation set for the Fully Successful level.
Unsatisfactory	Performs two or more tasks in a manner inconsistent with the expectations set for the Fully Successful level.

Index

Symbols

A

C

D

E

F

M

N

O

P

Q

R

S

T

U

W